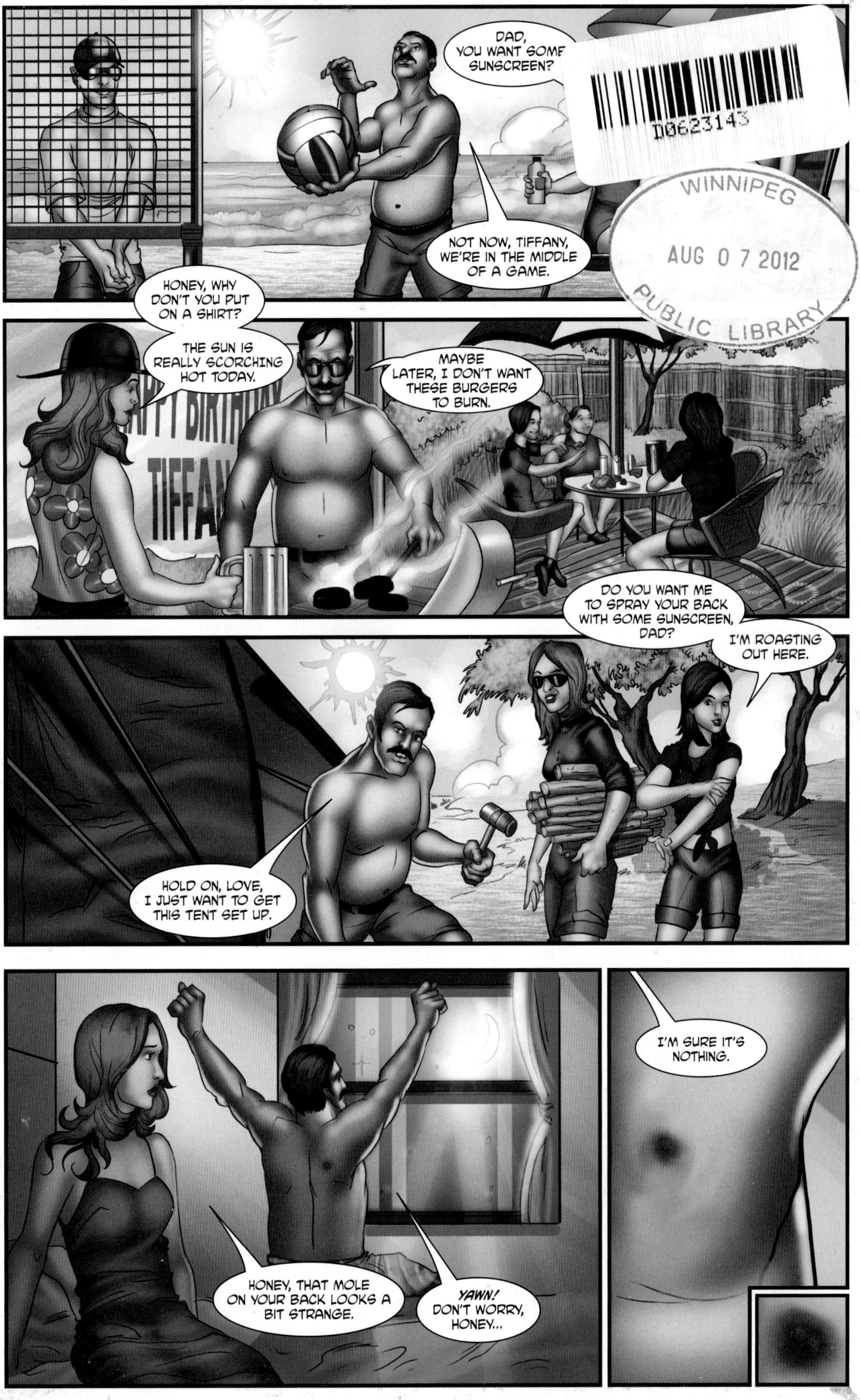
DAD, YOU WANT SOME SUNSCREEN?
NOT NOW, TIFFANY, WE'RE IN THE MIDDLE OF A GAME.
HONEY, WHY DON'T YOU PUT ON A SHIRT?
THE SUN IS REALLY SCORCHING HOT TODAY.
MAYBE LATER, I DON'T WANT THESE BURGERS TO BURN.
DO YOU WANT ME TO SPRAY YOUR BACK WITH SOME SUNSCREEN, DAD?
I'M ROASTING OUT HERE.
HOLD ON, LOVE, I JUST WANT TO GET THIS TENT SET UP.
HONEY, THAT MOLE ON YOUR BACK LOOKS A BIT STRANGE.
YAWN! DON'T WORRY, HONEY...
I'M SURE IT'S NOTHING.

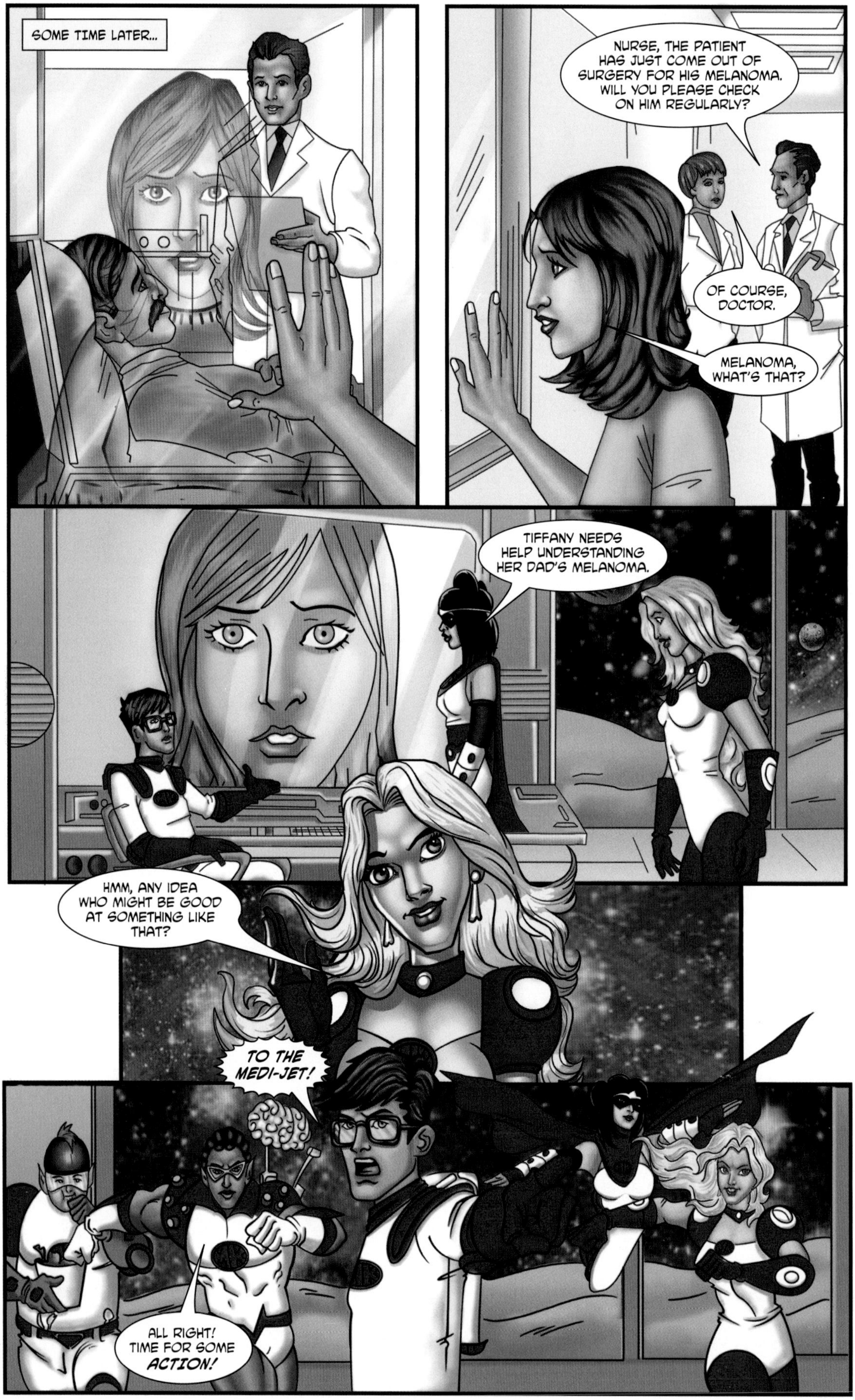
SOME TIME LATER...
NURSE, THE PATIENT HAS JUST COME OUT OF SURGERY FOR HIS MELANOMA. WILL YOU PLEASE CHECK ON HIM REGULARLY?
OF COURSE, DOCTOR.
MELANOMA, WHAT'S THAT?
TIFFANY NEEDS HELP UNDERSTANDING HER DAD'S MELANOMA.
HMM, ANY IDEA WHO MIGHT BE GOOD AT SOMETHING LIKE THAT?
TO THE MEDI-JET!
ALL RIGHT! TIME FOR SOME ACTION!

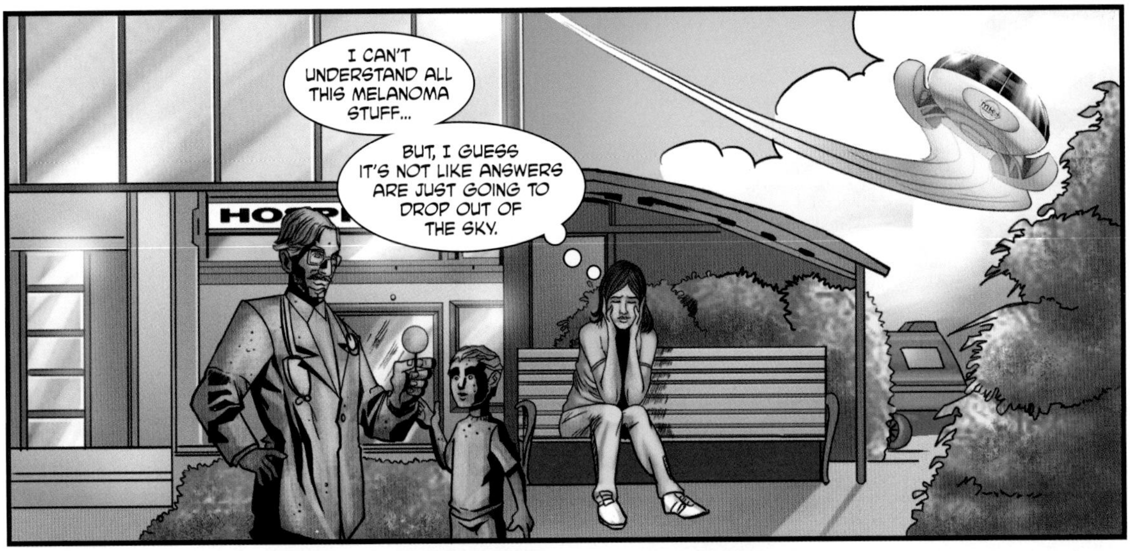
I CAN'T UNDERSTAND ALL THIS MELANOMA STUFF...
BUT, I GUESS IT'S NOT LIKE ANSWERS ARE JUST GOING TO DROP OUT OF THE SKY.

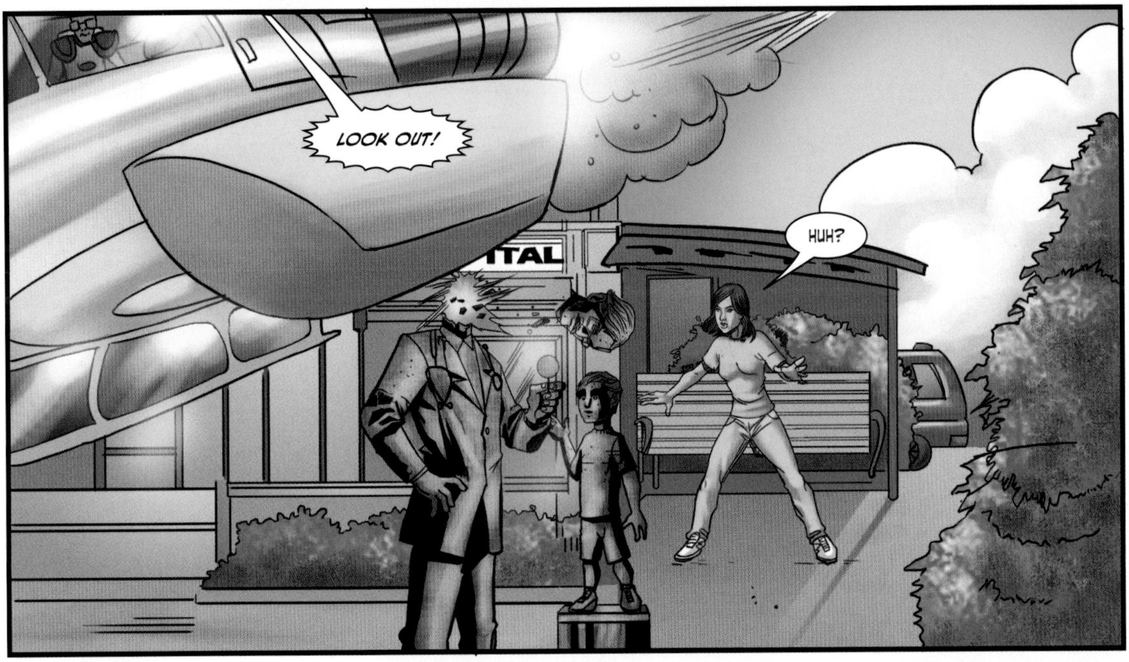
LOOK OUT!
HUH?

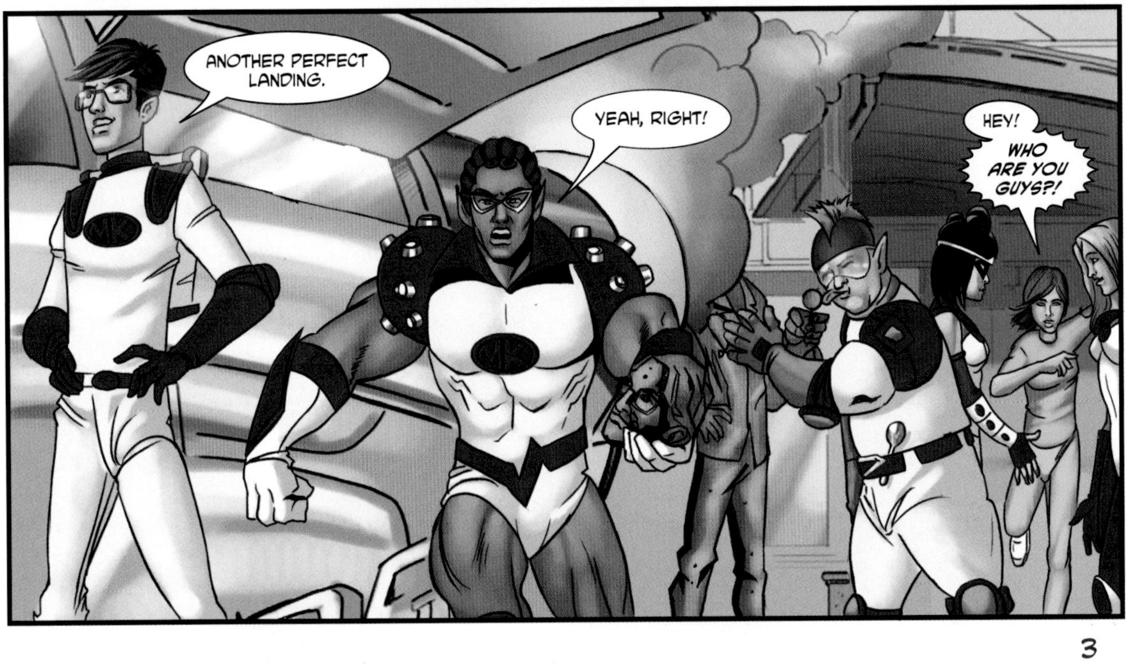
ANOTHER PERFECT LANDING.
YEAH, RIGHT!
HEY! WHO ARE YOU GUYS?!

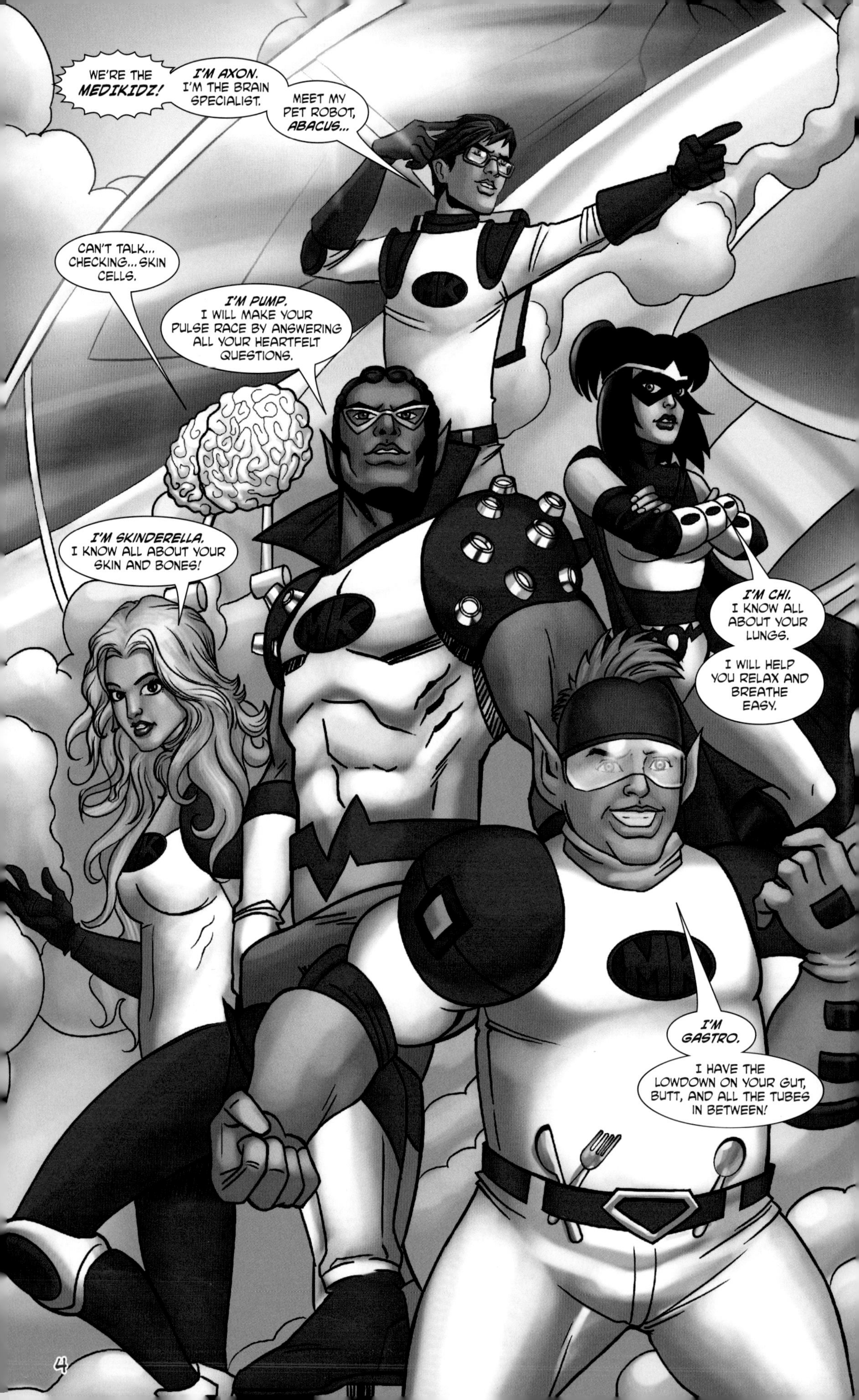
WE'RE THE MEDIKIDZ!
I'M AXON. I'M THE BRAIN SPECIALIST.
MEET MY PET ROBOT, ABACUS...
CAN'T TALK... CHECKING... SKIN CELLS.
I'M PUMP. I WILL MAKE YOUR PULSE RACE BY ANSWERING ALL YOUR HEARTFELT QUESTIONS.
I'M SKINDERELLA. I KNOW ALL ABOUT YOUR SKIN AND BONES!
I'M CHI. I KNOW ALL ABOUT YOUR LUNGS.
I WILL HELP YOU RELAX AND BREATHE EASY.
I'M GASTRO.
I HAVE THE LOWDOWN ON YOUR GUT, BUTT, AND ALL THE TUBES IN BETWEEN!

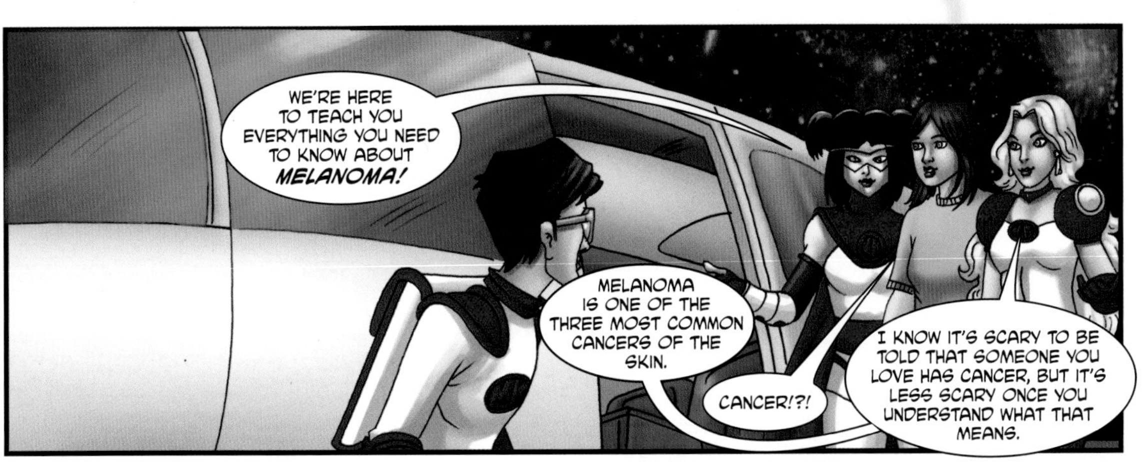
WE'RE HERE TO TEACH YOU EVERYTHING YOU NEED TO KNOW ABOUT *MELANOMA!*
MELANOMA IS ONE OF THE THREE MOST COMMON CANCERS OF THE SKIN.
CANCER!?!
I KNOW IT'S SCARY TO BE TOLD THAT SOMEONE YOU LOVE HAS CANCER, BUT IT'S LESS SCARY ONCE YOU UNDERSTAND WHAT THAT MEANS.

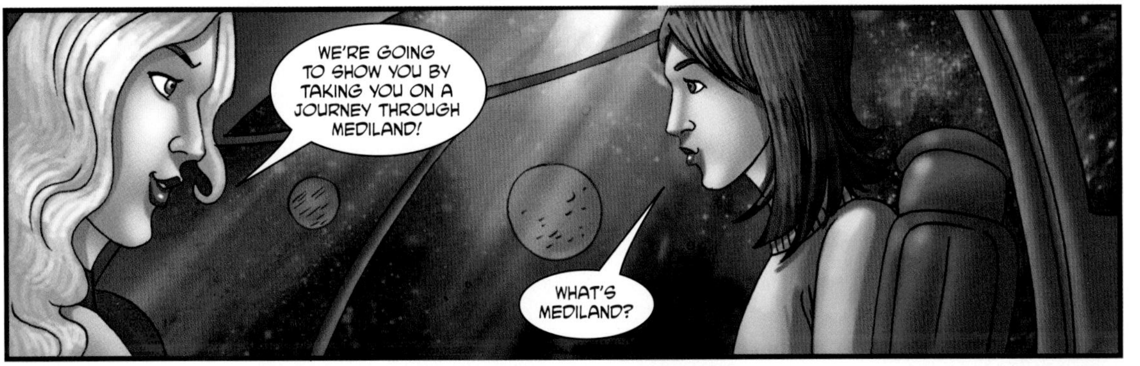
WE'RE GOING TO SHOW YOU BY TAKING YOU ON A JOURNEY THROUGH MEDILAND!
WHAT'S MEDILAND?

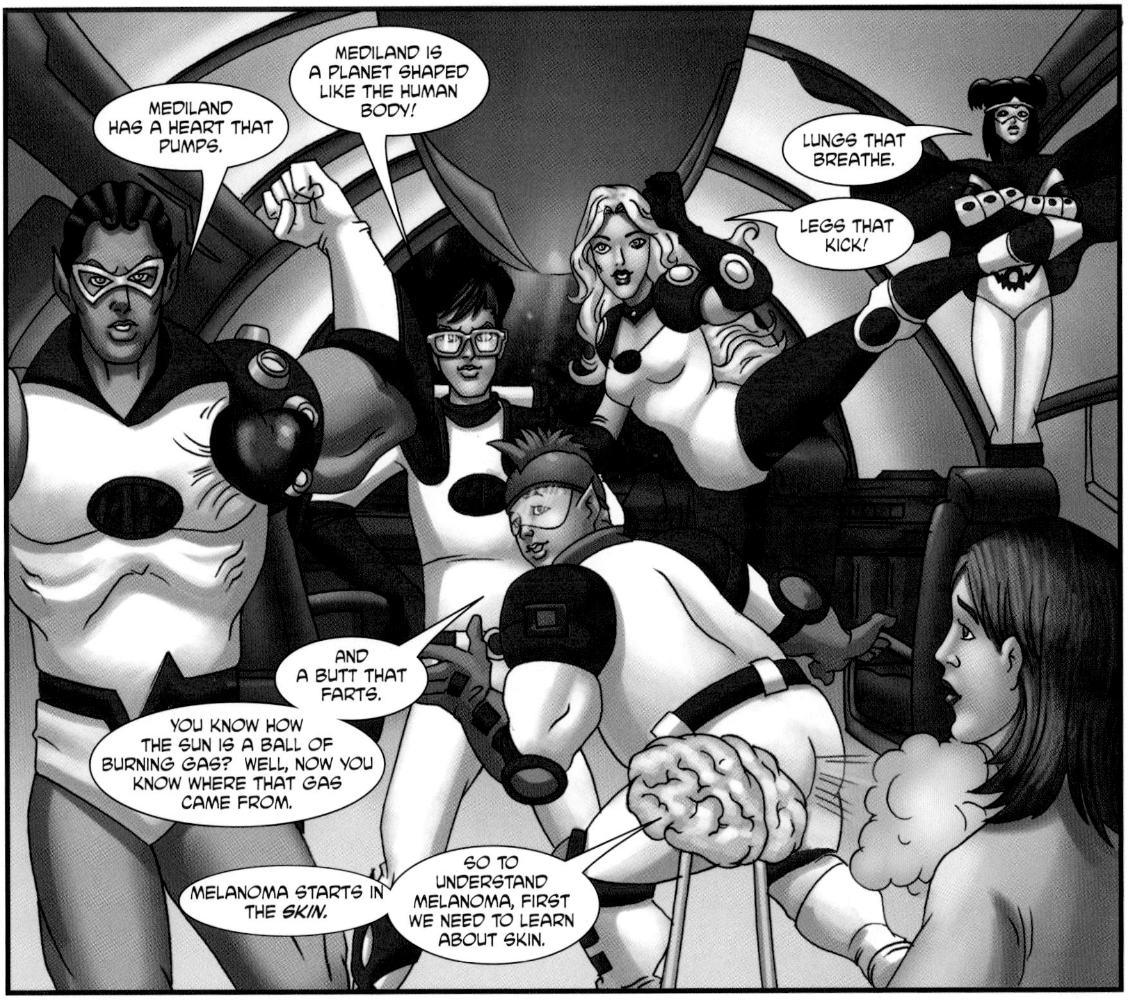
MEDILAND IS A PLANET SHAPED LIKE THE HUMAN BODY!
MEDILAND HAS A HEART THAT PUMPS.
LUNGS THAT BREATHE.
LEGS THAT KICK!
AND A BUTT THAT FARTS.
YOU KNOW HOW THE SUN IS A BALL OF BURNING GAS? WELL, NOW YOU KNOW WHERE THAT GAS CAME FROM.
MELANOMA STARTS IN THE *SKIN.*
SO TO UNDERSTAND MELANOMA, FIRST WE NEED TO LEARN ABOUT SKIN.

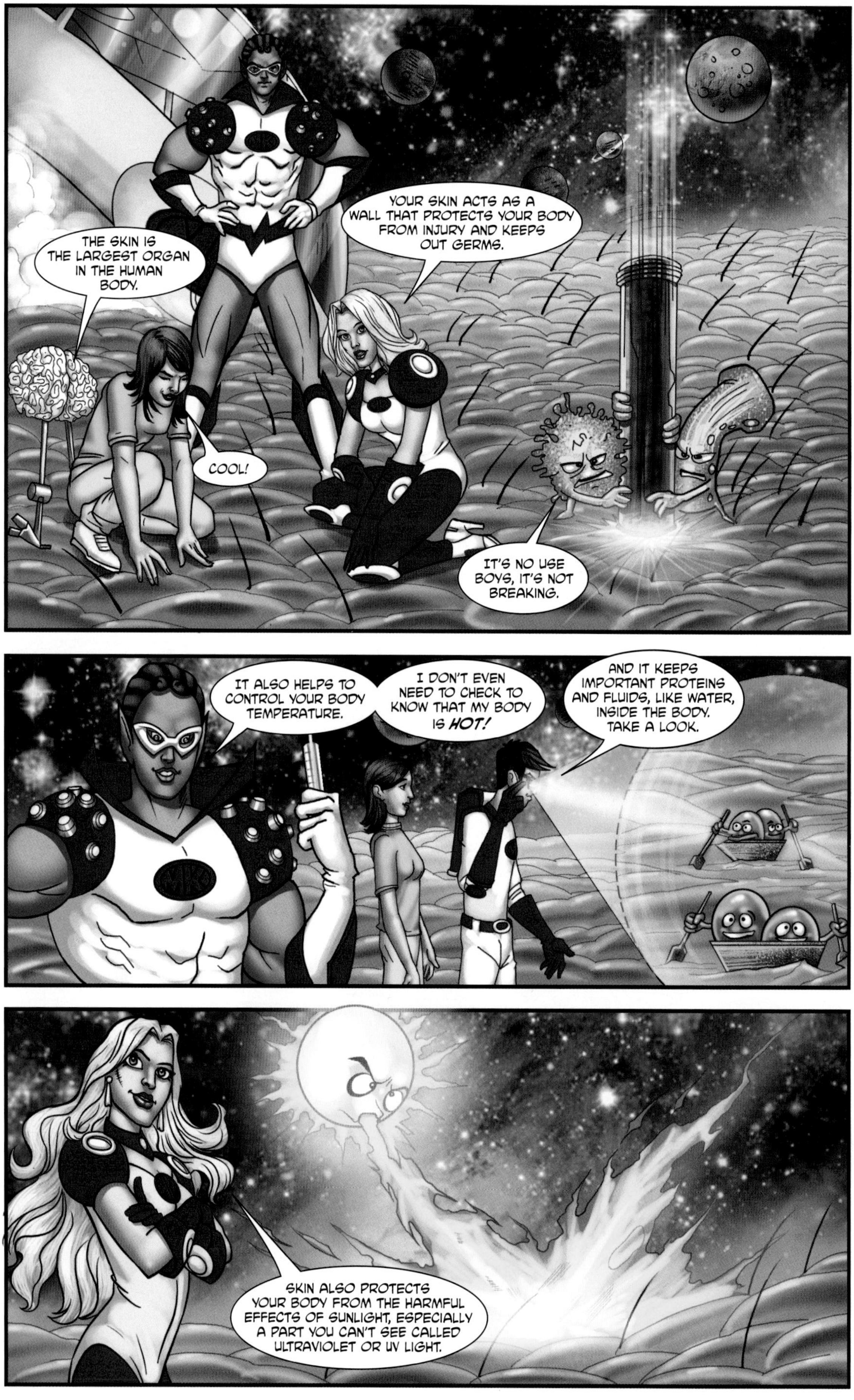
THE SKIN IS THE LARGEST ORGAN IN THE HUMAN BODY.
YOUR SKIN ACTS AS A WALL THAT PROTECTS YOUR BODY FROM INJURY AND KEEPS OUT GERMS.
COOL!
IT'S NO USE BOYS, IT'S NOT BREAKING.
IT ALSO HELPS TO CONTROL YOUR BODY TEMPERATURE.
I DON'T EVEN NEED TO CHECK TO KNOW THAT MY BODY IS ***HOT!***
AND IT KEEPS IMPORTANT PROTEINS AND FLUIDS, LIKE WATER, INSIDE THE BODY. TAKE A LOOK.
SKIN ALSO PROTECTS YOUR BODY FROM THE HARMFUL EFFECTS OF SUNLIGHT, ESPECIALLY A PART YOU CAN'T SEE CALLED ULTRAVIOLET OR UV LIGHT.

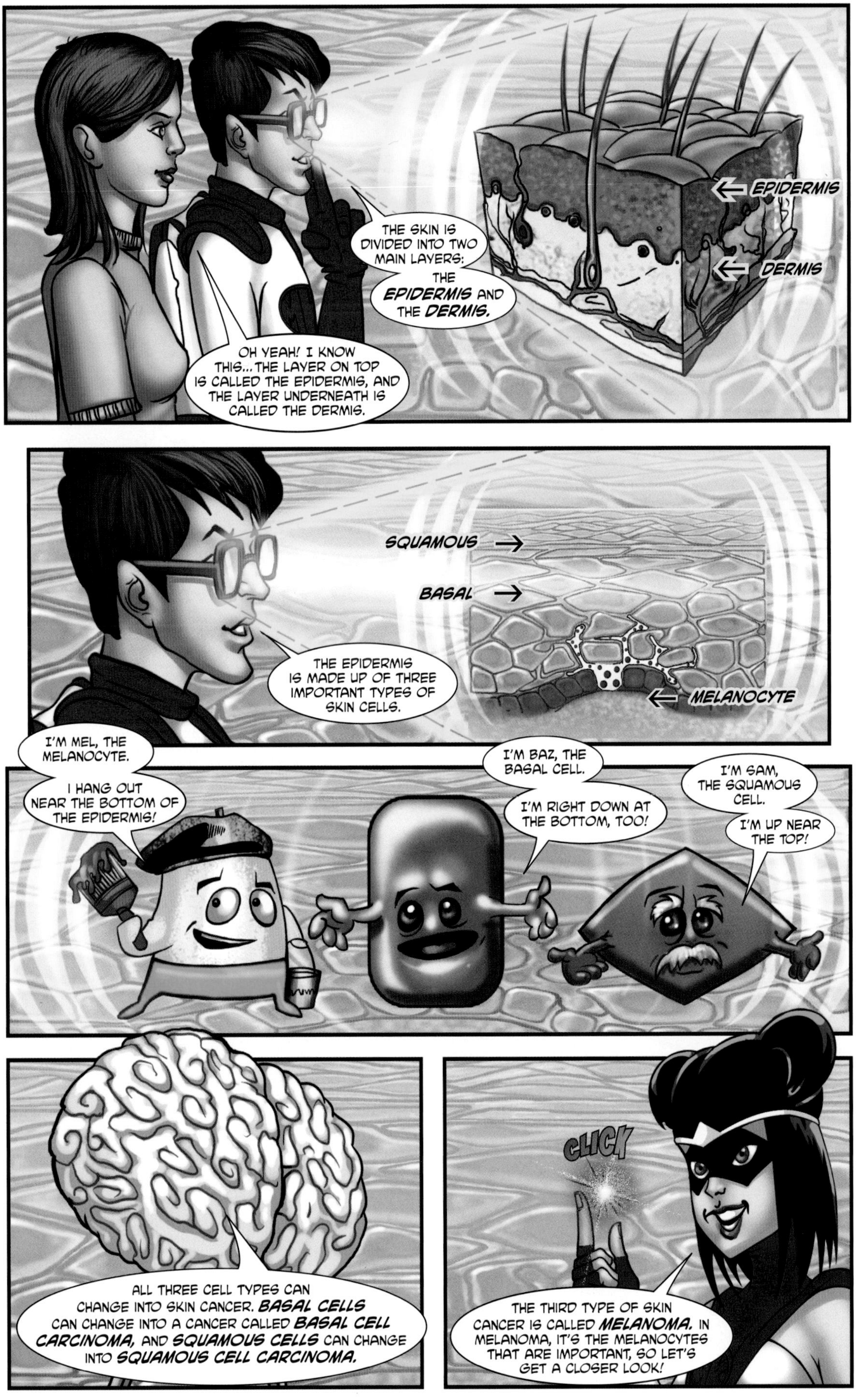
THE SKIN IS DIVIDED INTO TWO MAIN LAYERS:
THE EPIDERMIS AND THE DERMIS.
EPIDERMIS
DERMIS
OH YEAH! I KNOW THIS...THE LAYER ON TOP IS CALLED THE EPIDERMIS, AND THE LAYER UNDERNEATH IS CALLED THE DERMIS.
SQUAMOUS
BASAL
MELANOCYTE
THE EPIDERMIS IS MADE UP OF THREE IMPORTANT TYPES OF SKIN CELLS.
I'M MEL, THE MELANOCYTE.
I HANG OUT NEAR THE BOTTOM OF THE EPIDERMIS!
I'M BAZ, THE BASAL CELL.
I'M RIGHT DOWN AT THE BOTTOM, TOO!
I'M SAM, THE SQUAMOUS CELL.
I'M UP NEAR THE TOP!
ALL THREE CELL TYPES CAN CHANGE INTO SKIN CANCER. BASAL CELLS CAN CHANGE INTO A CANCER CALLED BASAL CELL CARCINOMA, AND SQUAMOUS CELLS CAN CHANGE INTO SQUAMOUS CELL CARCINOMA.
CLICK
THE THIRD TYPE OF SKIN CANCER IS CALLED MELANOMA. IN MELANOMA, IT'S THE MELANOCYTES THAT ARE IMPORTANT, SO LET'S GET A CLOSER LOOK!

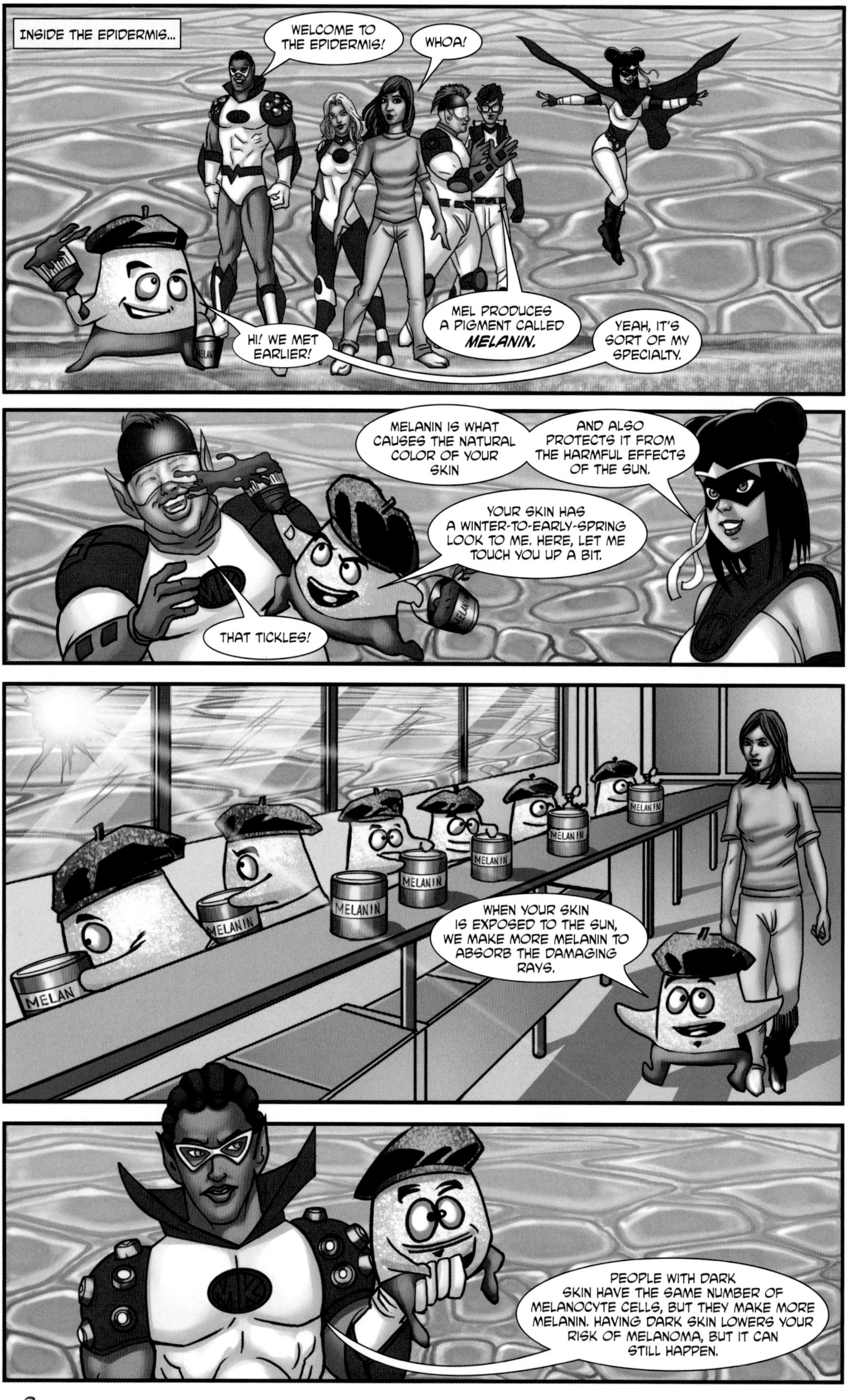
INSIDE THE EPIDERMIS...
WELCOME TO THE EPIDERMIS!
WHOA!
HI! WE MET EARLIER!
MEL PRODUCES A PIGMENT CALLED *MELANIN.*
YEAH, IT'S SORT OF MY SPECIALTY.
MELANIN IS WHAT CAUSES THE NATURAL COLOR OF YOUR SKIN
AND ALSO PROTECTS IT FROM THE HARMFUL EFFECTS OF THE SUN.
YOUR SKIN HAS A WINTER-TO-EARLY-SPRING LOOK TO ME. HERE, LET ME TOUCH YOU UP A BIT.
THAT TICKLES!
MELANIN
WHEN YOUR SKIN IS EXPOSED TO THE SUN, WE MAKE MORE MELANIN TO ABSORB THE DAMAGING RAYS.
PEOPLE WITH DARK SKIN HAVE THE SAME NUMBER OF MELANOCYTE CELLS, BUT THEY MAKE MORE MELANIN. HAVING DARK SKIN LOWERS YOUR RISK OF MELANOMA, BUT IT CAN STILL HAPPEN.

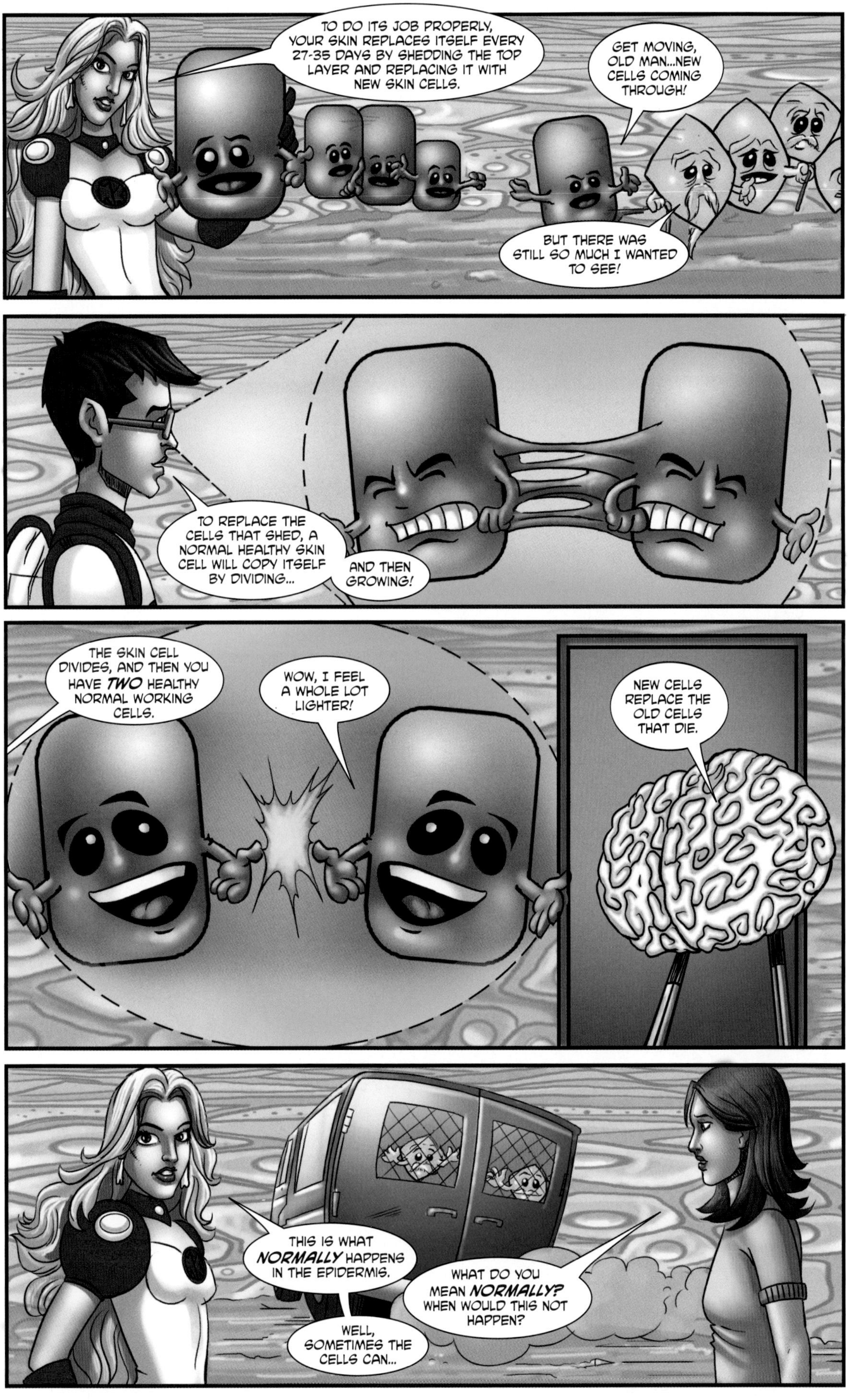
TO DO ITS JOB PROPERLY, YOUR SKIN REPLACES ITSELF EVERY 27-35 DAYS BY SHEDDING THE TOP LAYER AND REPLACING IT WITH NEW SKIN CELLS.
GET MOVING, OLD MAN...NEW CELLS COMING THROUGH!
BUT THERE WAS STILL SO MUCH I WANTED TO SEE!
TO REPLACE THE CELLS THAT SHED, A NORMAL HEALTHY SKIN CELL WILL COPY ITSELF BY DIVIDING...
AND THEN GROWING!
THE SKIN CELL DIVIDES, AND THEN YOU HAVE TWO HEALTHY NORMAL WORKING CELLS.
WOW, I FEEL A WHOLE LOT LIGHTER!
NEW CELLS REPLACE THE OLD CELLS THAT DIE.
THIS IS WHAT NORMALLY HAPPENS IN THE EPIDERMIS.
WHAT DO YOU MEAN NORMALLY? WHEN WOULD THIS NOT HAPPEN?
WELL, SOMETIMES THE CELLS CAN...

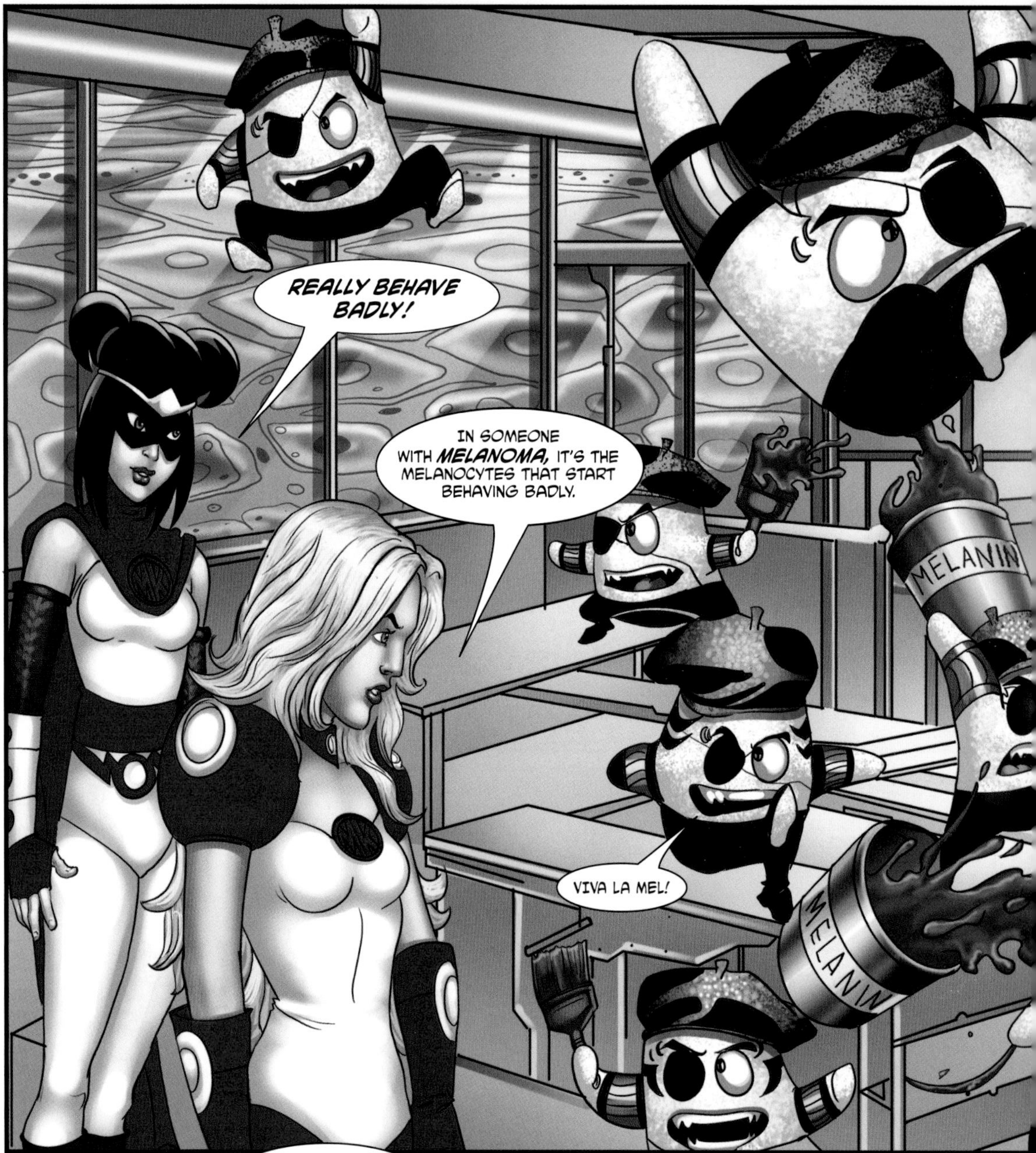
REALLY BEHAVE BADLY!
IN SOMEONE WITH MELANOMA, IT'S THE MELANOCYTES THAT START BEHAVING BADLY.
MELANIN
VIVA LA MEL!
MELANIN

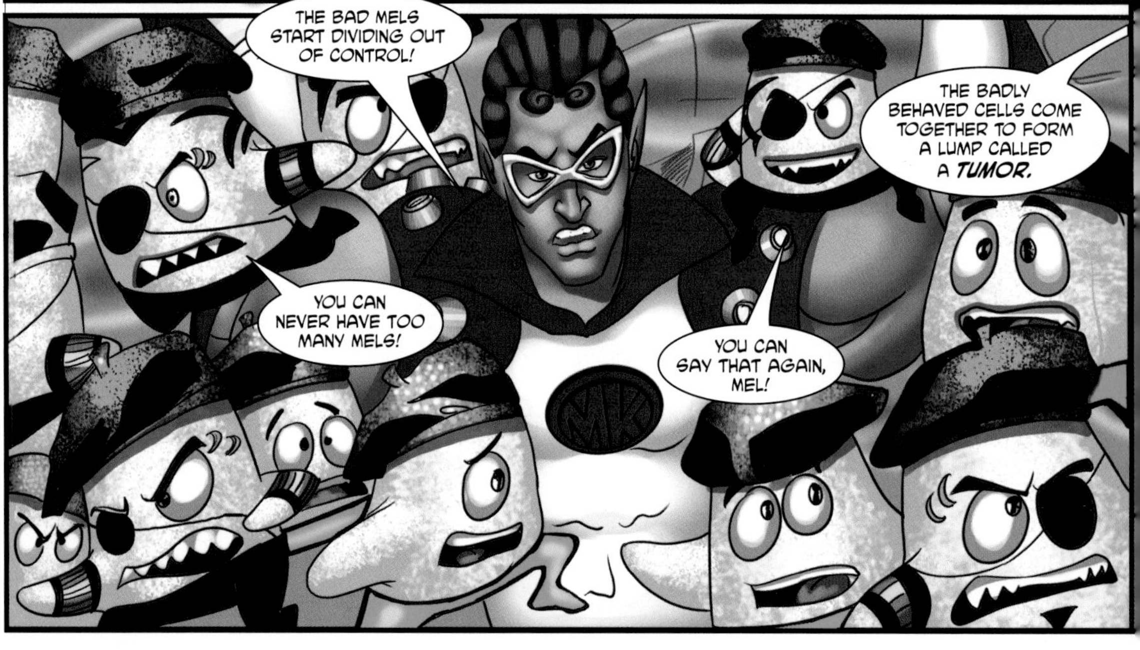
THE BAD MELS START DIVIDING OUT OF CONTROL!
THE BADLY BEHAVED CELLS COME TOGETHER TO FORM A LUMP CALLED A TUMOR.
YOU CAN NEVER HAVE TOO MANY MELS!
YOU CAN SAY THAT AGAIN, MEL!

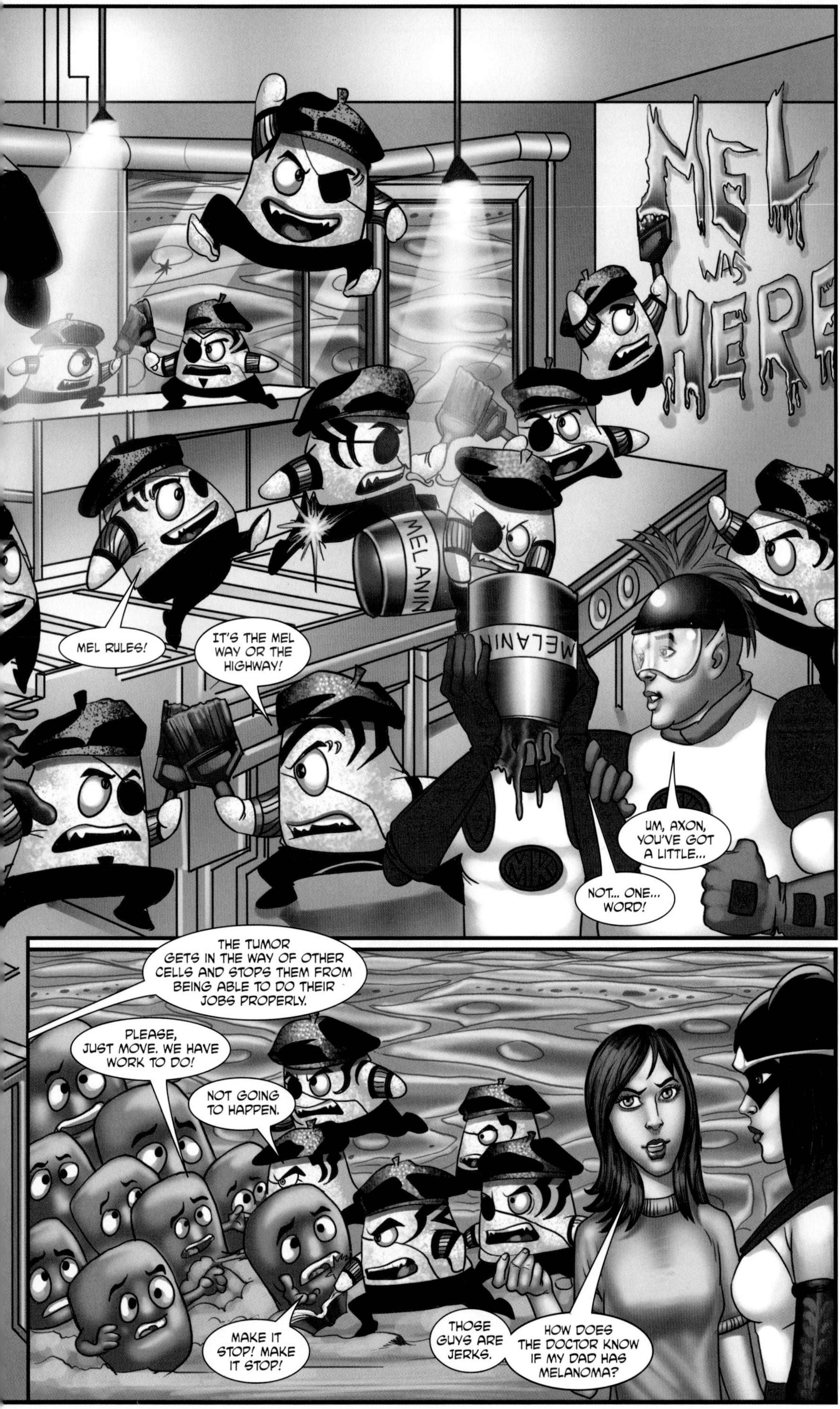
MEL WAS HERE
MEL RULES!
IT'S THE MEL WAY OR THE HIGHWAY!
MELANIN
MELANIN
UM, AXON, YOU'VE GOT A LITTLE...
NOT... ONE... WORD!
THE TUMOR GETS IN THE WAY OF OTHER CELLS AND STOPS THEM FROM BEING ABLE TO DO THEIR JOBS PROPERLY.
PLEASE, JUST MOVE. WE HAVE WORK TO DO!
NOT GOING TO HAPPEN.
MAKE IT STOP! MAKE IT STOP!
THOSE GUYS ARE JERKS.
HOW DOES THE DOCTOR KNOW IF MY DAD HAS MELANOMA?

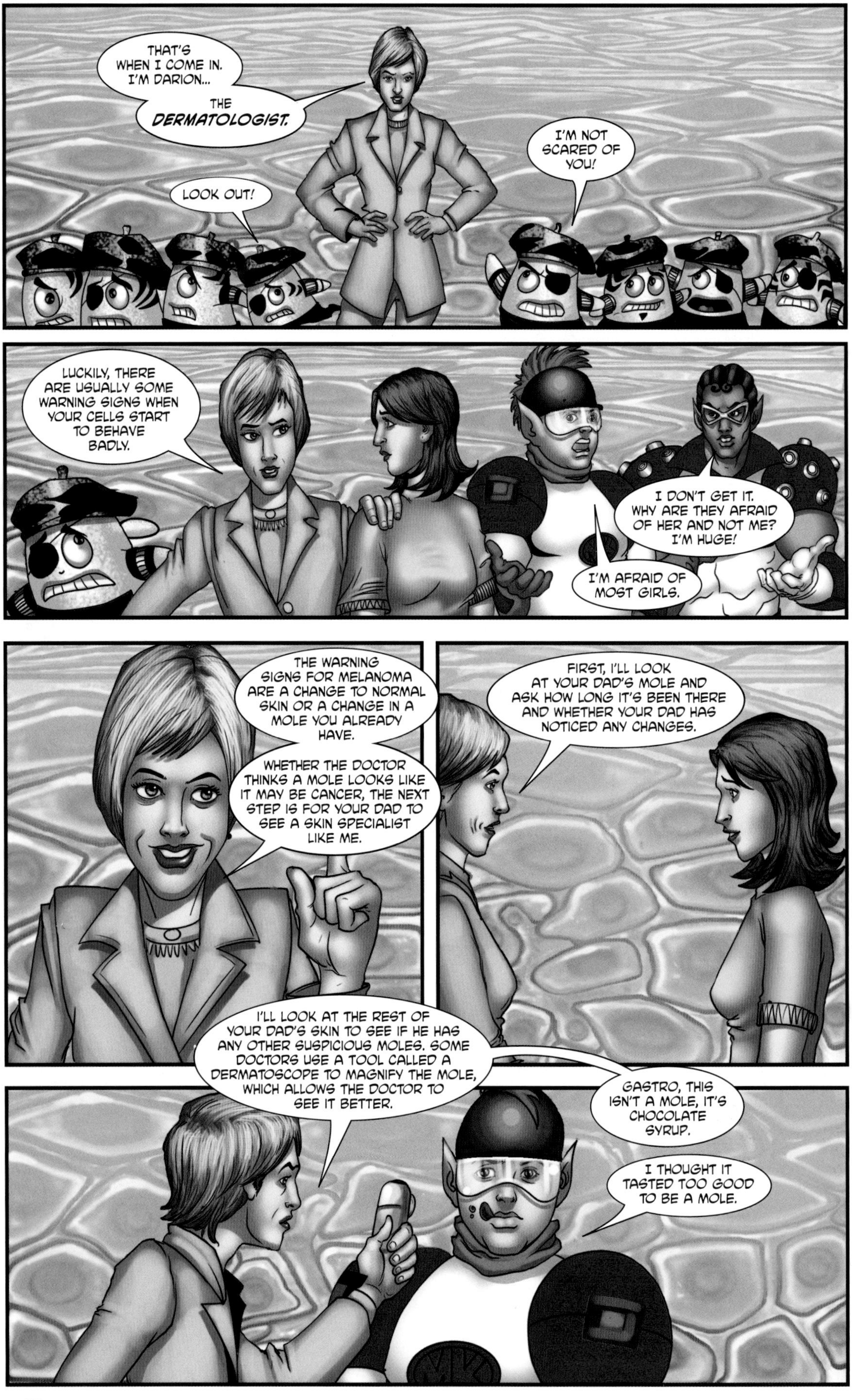
THAT'S WHEN I COME IN. I'M DARION... THE DERMATOLOGIST.
LOOK OUT!
I'M NOT SCARED OF YOU!
LUCKILY, THERE ARE USUALLY SOME WARNING SIGNS WHEN YOUR CELLS START TO BEHAVE BADLY.
I DON'T GET IT. WHY ARE THEY AFRAID OF HER AND NOT ME? I'M HUGE!
I'M AFRAID OF MOST GIRLS.
THE WARNING SIGNS FOR MELANOMA ARE A CHANGE TO NORMAL SKIN OR A CHANGE IN A MOLE YOU ALREADY HAVE.
WHETHER THE DOCTOR THINKS A MOLE LOOKS LIKE IT MAY BE CANCER, THE NEXT STEP IS FOR YOUR DAD TO SEE A SKIN SPECIALIST LIKE ME.
FIRST, I'LL LOOK AT YOUR DAD'S MOLE AND ASK HOW LONG IT'S BEEN THERE AND WHETHER YOUR DAD HAS NOTICED ANY CHANGES.
I'LL LOOK AT THE REST OF YOUR DAD'S SKIN TO SEE IF HE HAS ANY OTHER SUSPICIOUS MOLES. SOME DOCTORS USE A TOOL CALLED A DERMATOSCOPE TO MAGNIFY THE MOLE, WHICH ALLOWS THE DOCTOR TO SEE IT BETTER.
GASTRO, THIS ISN'T A MOLE, IT'S CHOCOLATE SYRUP.
I THOUGHT IT TASTED TOO GOOD TO BE A MOLE.

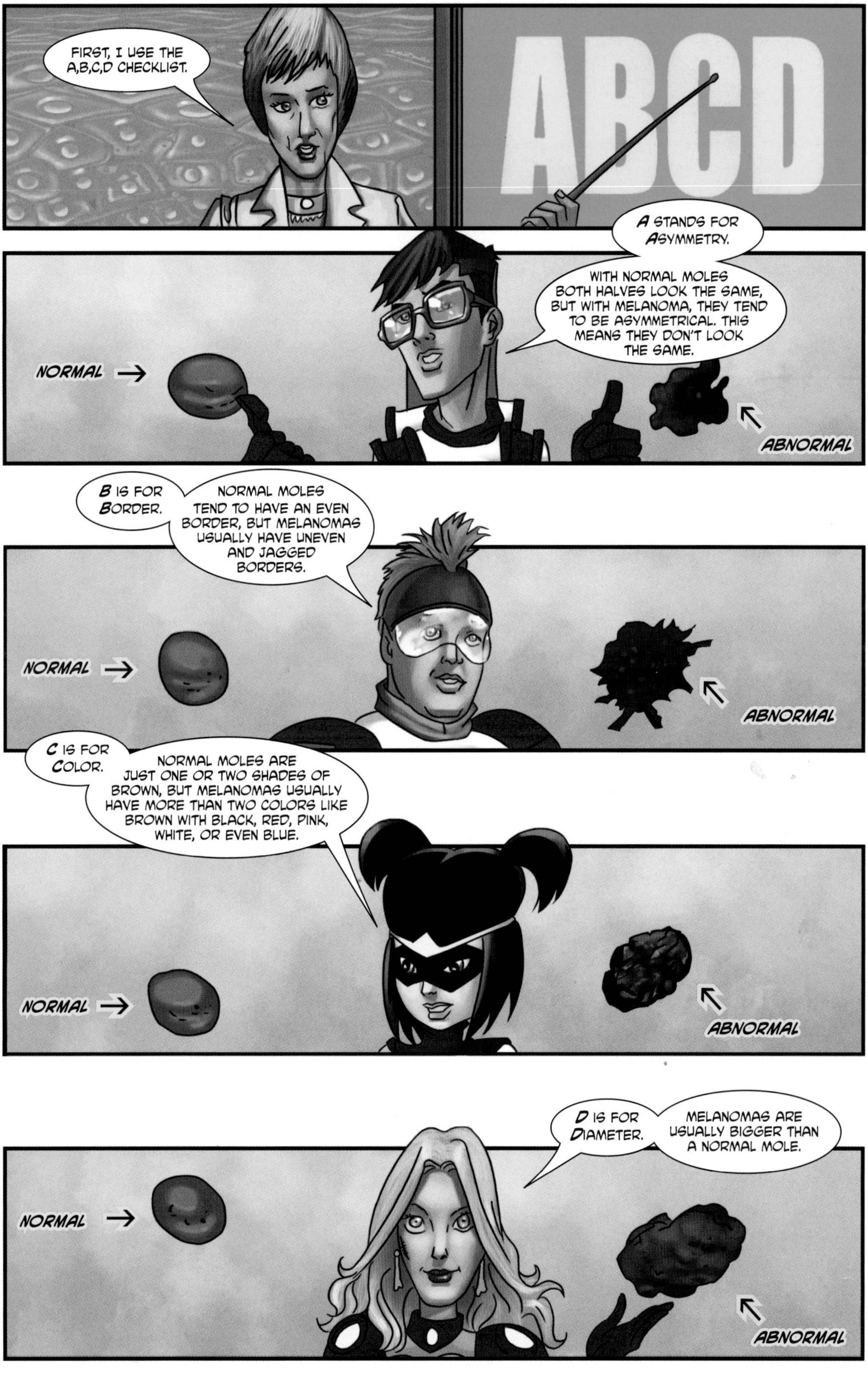
FIRST, I USE THE A,B,C,D CHECKLIST.
ABCD
A STANDS FOR ASYMMETRY.
WITH NORMAL MOLES BOTH HALVES LOOK THE SAME, BUT WITH MELANOMA, THEY TEND TO BE ASYMMETRICAL. THIS MEANS THEY DON'T LOOK THE SAME.
NORMAL
ABNORMAL
B IS FOR BORDER.
NORMAL MOLES TEND TO HAVE AN EVEN BORDER, BUT MELANOMAS USUALLY HAVE UNEVEN AND JAGGED BORDERS.
NORMAL
ABNORMAL
C IS FOR COLOR.
NORMAL MOLES ARE JUST ONE OR TWO SHADES OF BROWN, BUT MELANOMAS USUALLY HAVE MORE THAN TWO COLORS LIKE BROWN WITH BLACK, RED, PINK, WHITE, OR EVEN BLUE.
NORMAL
ABNORMAL
D IS FOR DIAMETER.
MELANOMAS ARE USUALLY BIGGER THAN A NORMAL MOLE.
NORMAL
ABNORMAL

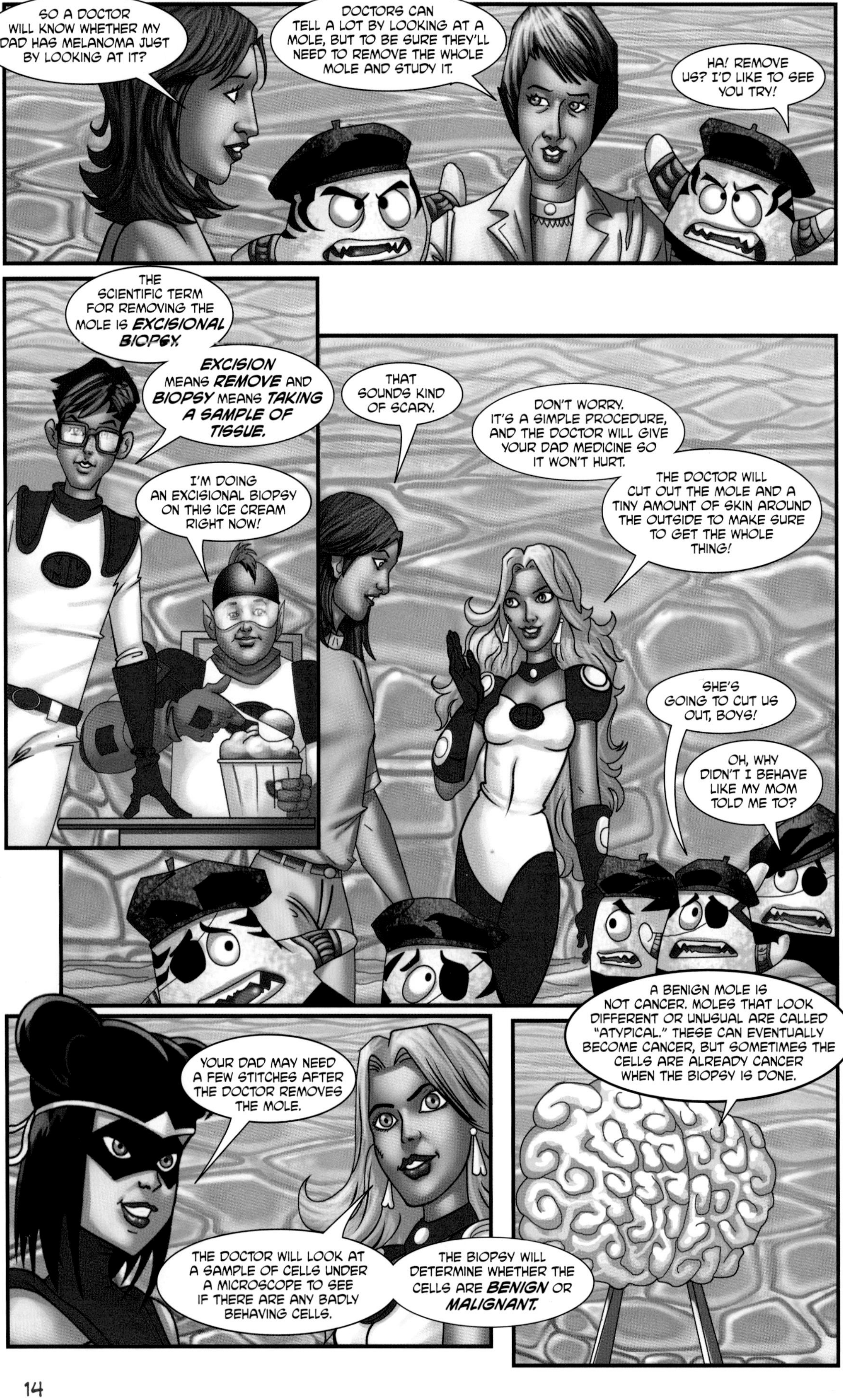
SO A DOCTOR WILL KNOW WHETHER MY DAD HAS MELANOMA JUST BY LOOKING AT IT?
DOCTORS CAN TELL A LOT BY LOOKING AT A MOLE, BUT TO BE SURE THEY'LL NEED TO REMOVE THE WHOLE MOLE AND STUDY IT.
HA! REMOVE US? I'D LIKE TO SEE YOU TRY!
THE SCIENTIFIC TERM FOR REMOVING THE MOLE IS EXCISIONAL BIOPSY.
EXCISION MEANS REMOVE AND BIOPSY MEANS TAKING A SAMPLE OF TISSUE.
I'M DOING AN EXCISIONAL BIOPSY ON THIS ICE CREAM RIGHT NOW!
THAT SOUNDS KIND OF SCARY.
DON'T WORRY. IT'S A SIMPLE PROCEDURE, AND THE DOCTOR WILL GIVE YOUR DAD MEDICINE SO IT WON'T HURT.
THE DOCTOR WILL CUT OUT THE MOLE AND A TINY AMOUNT OF SKIN AROUND THE OUTSIDE TO MAKE SURE TO GET THE WHOLE THING!
SHE'S GOING TO CUT US OUT, BOYS!
OH, WHY DIDN'T I BEHAVE LIKE MY MOM TOLD ME TO?
YOUR DAD MAY NEED A FEW STITCHES AFTER THE DOCTOR REMOVES THE MOLE.
THE DOCTOR WILL LOOK AT A SAMPLE OF CELLS UNDER A MICROSCOPE TO SEE IF THERE ARE ANY BADLY BEHAVING CELLS.
THE BIOPSY WILL DETERMINE WHETHER THE CELLS ARE BENIGN OR MALIGNANT.
A BENIGN MOLE IS NOT CANCER. MOLES THAT LOOK DIFFERENT OR UNUSUAL ARE CALLED "ATYPICAL." THESE CAN EVENTUALLY BECOME CANCER, BUT SOMETIMES THE CELLS ARE ALREADY CANCER WHEN THE BIOPSY IS DONE.

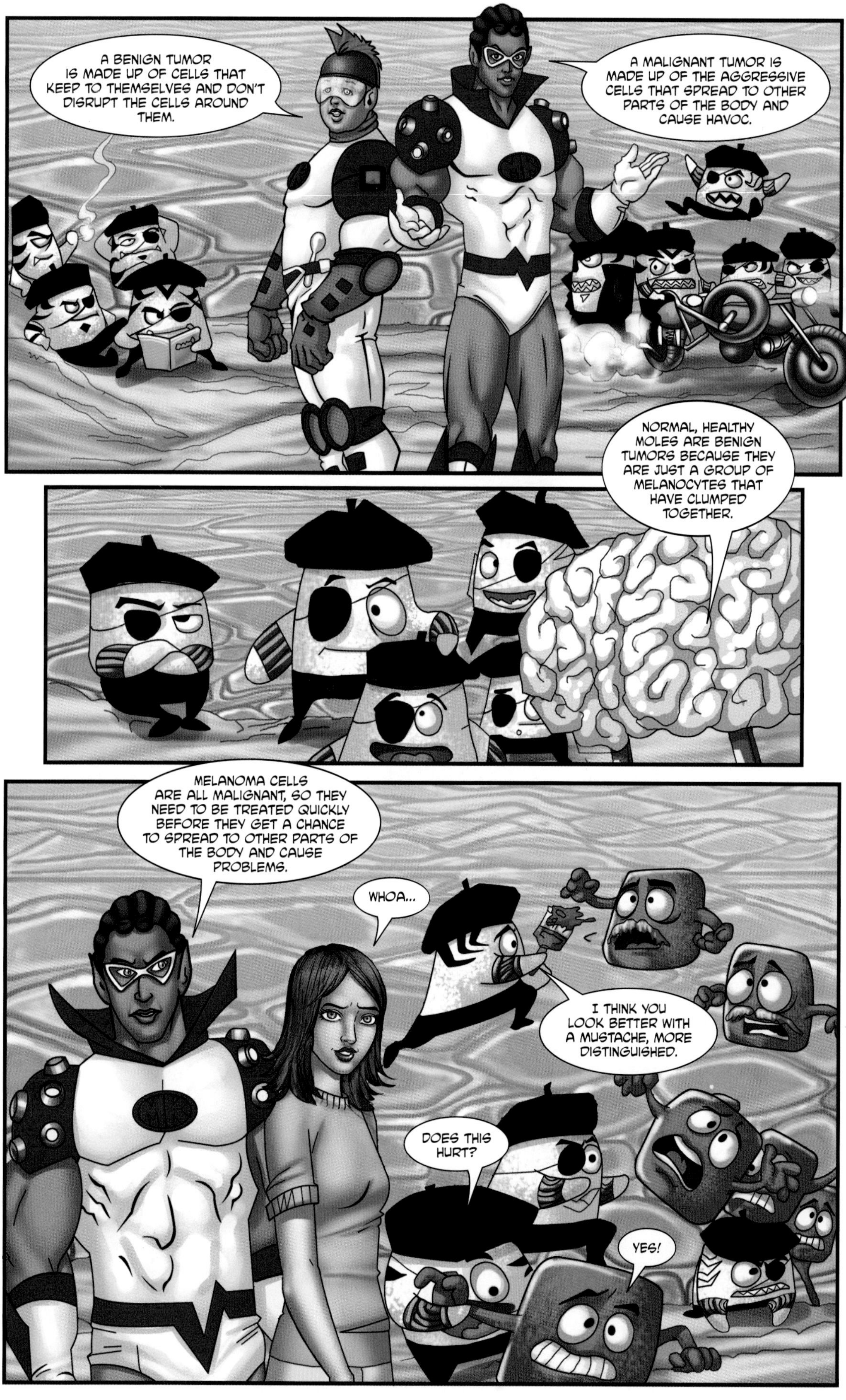
A BENIGN TUMOR IS MADE UP OF CELLS THAT KEEP TO THEMSELVES AND DON'T DISRUPT THE CELLS AROUND THEM.
A MALIGNANT TUMOR IS MADE UP OF THE AGGRESSIVE CELLS THAT SPREAD TO OTHER PARTS OF THE BODY AND CAUSE HAVOC.
NORMAL, HEALTHY MOLES ARE BENIGN TUMORS BECAUSE THEY ARE JUST A GROUP OF MELANOCYTES THAT HAVE CLUMPED TOGETHER.
MELANOMA CELLS ARE ALL MALIGNANT, SO THEY NEED TO BE TREATED QUICKLY BEFORE THEY GET A CHANCE TO SPREAD TO OTHER PARTS OF THE BODY AND CAUSE PROBLEMS.
WHOA...
I THINK YOU LOOK BETTER WITH A MUSTACHE, MORE DISTINGUISHED.
DOES THIS HURT?
YES!

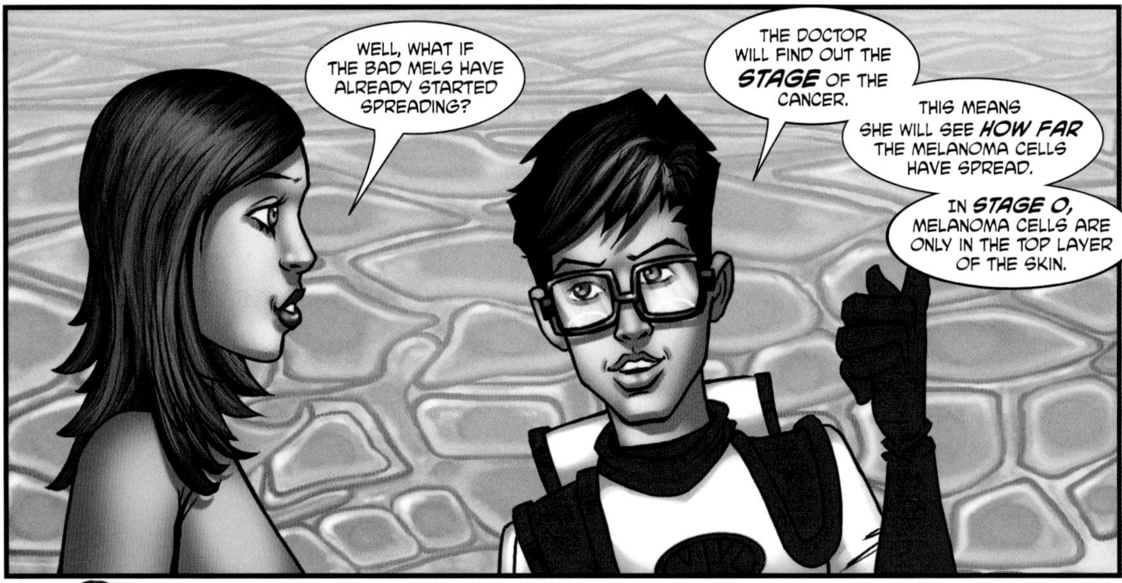
WELL, WHAT IF THE BAD MELS HAVE ALREADY STARTED SPREADING?
THE DOCTOR WILL FIND OUT THE ***STAGE*** OF THE CANCER.
THIS MEANS SHE WILL SEE ***HOW FAR*** THE MELANOMA CELLS HAVE SPREAD.
IN ***STAGE 0,*** MELANOMA CELLS ARE ONLY IN THE TOP LAYER OF THE SKIN.

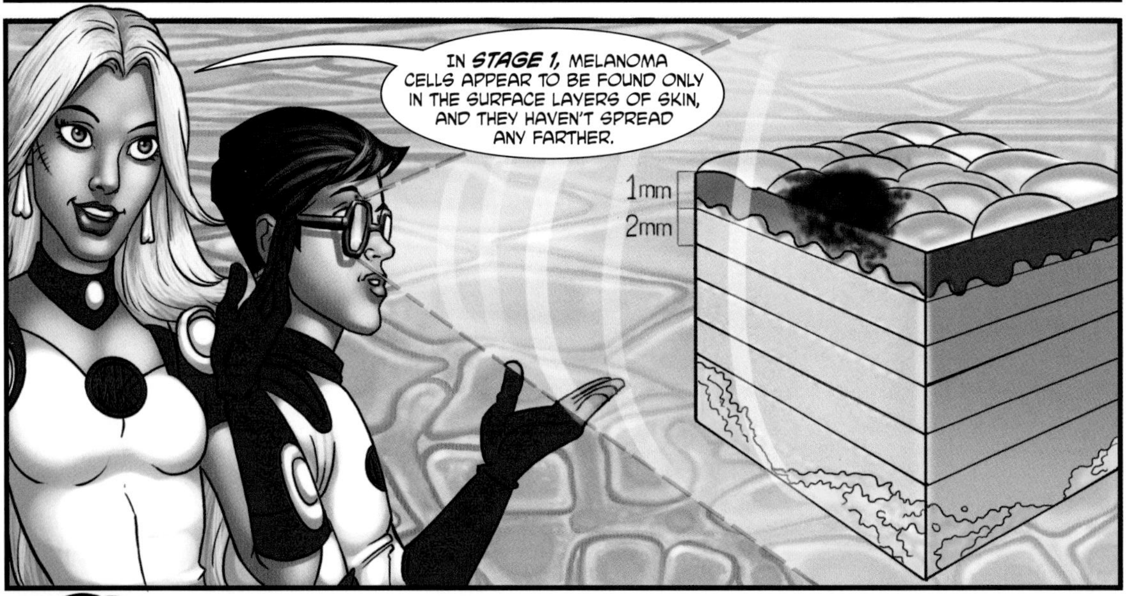
IN ***STAGE 1,*** MELANOMA CELLS APPEAR TO BE FOUND ONLY IN THE SURFACE LAYERS OF SKIN, AND THEY HAVEN'T SPREAD ANY FARTHER.
1mm
2mm

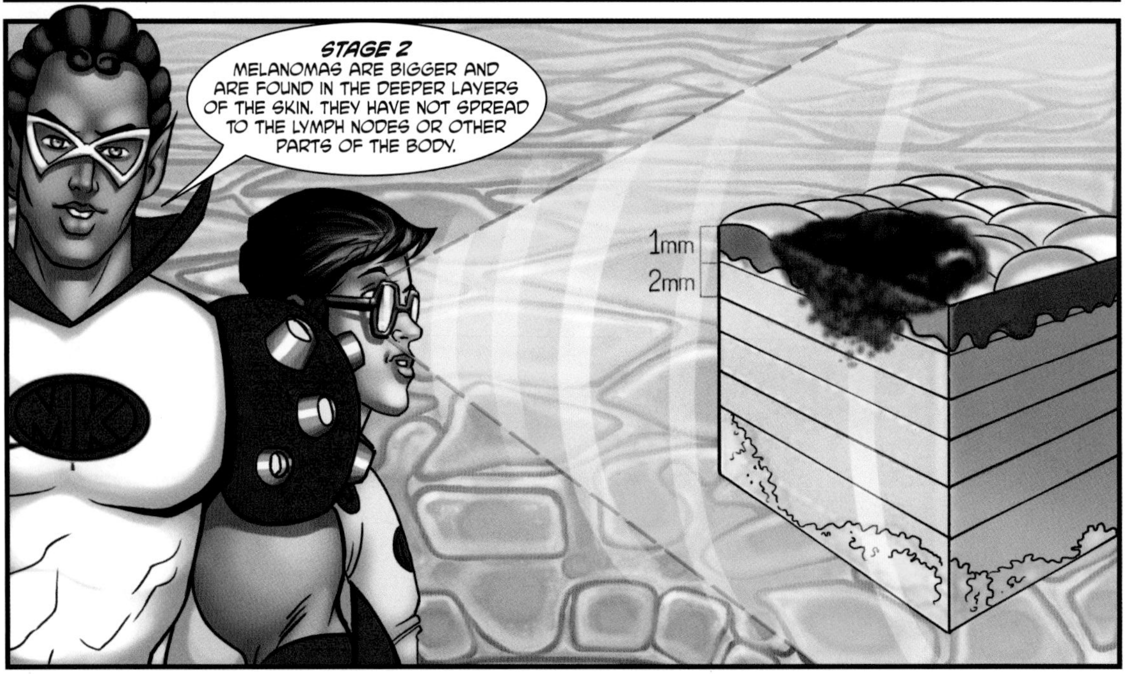
STAGE 2 MELANOMAS ARE BIGGER AND ARE FOUND IN THE DEEPER LAYERS OF THE SKIN. THEY HAVE NOT SPREAD TO THE LYMPH NODES OR OTHER PARTS OF THE BODY.
1mm
2mm

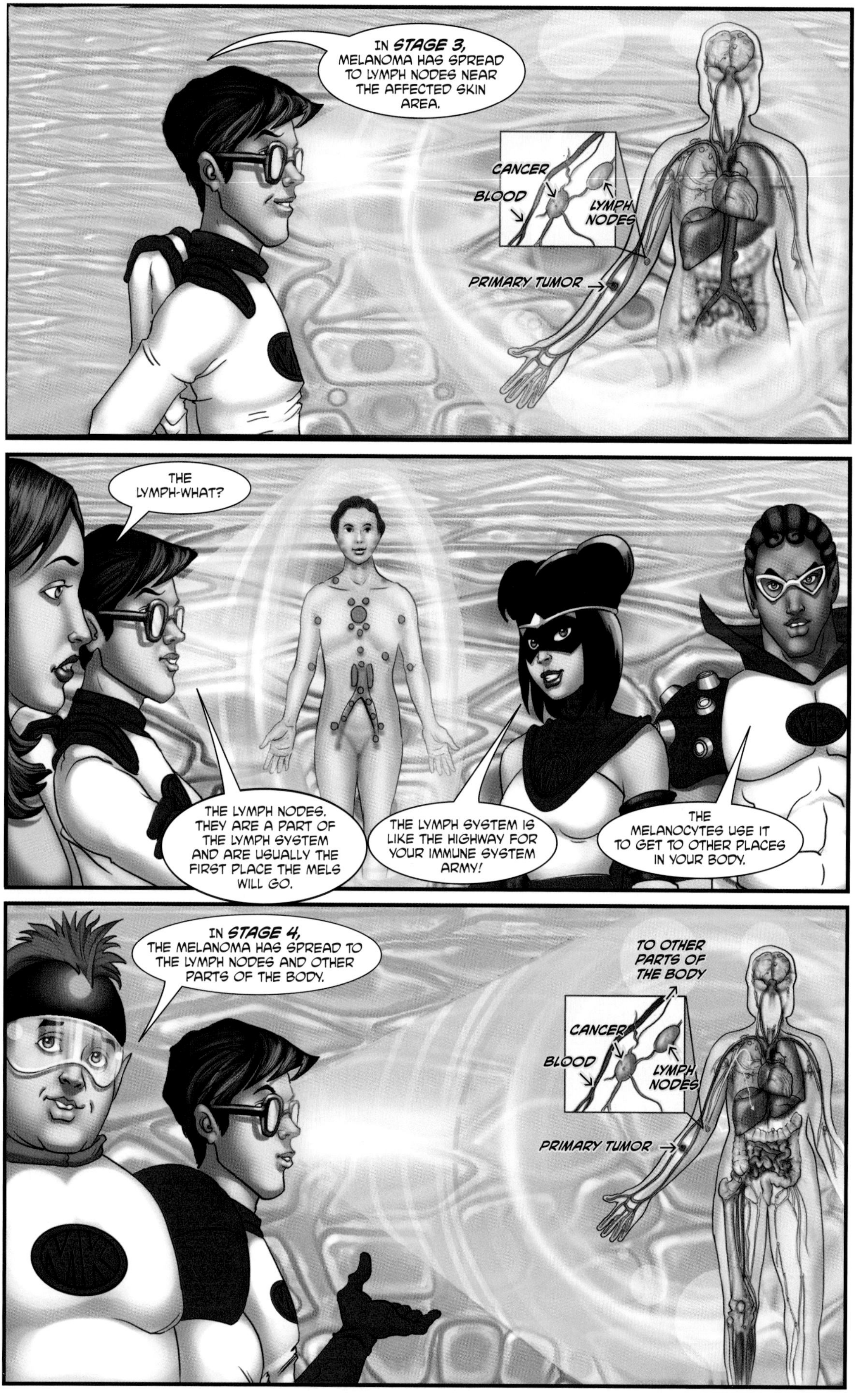
IN STAGE 3, MELANOMA HAS SPREAD TO LYMPH NODES NEAR THE AFFECTED SKIN AREA.
CANCER
BLOOD
LYMPH NODES
PRIMARY TUMOR
THE LYMPH-WHAT?
THE LYMPH NODES. THEY ARE A PART OF THE LYMPH SYSTEM AND ARE USUALLY THE FIRST PLACE THE MELS WILL GO.
THE LYMPH SYSTEM IS LIKE THE HIGHWAY FOR YOUR IMMUNE SYSTEM ARMY!
THE MELANOCYTES USE IT TO GET TO OTHER PLACES IN YOUR BODY.
IN STAGE 4, THE MELANOMA HAS SPREAD TO THE LYMPH NODES AND OTHER PARTS OF THE BODY.
TO OTHER PARTS OF THE BODY
CANCER
BLOOD
LYMPH NODES
PRIMARY TUMOR

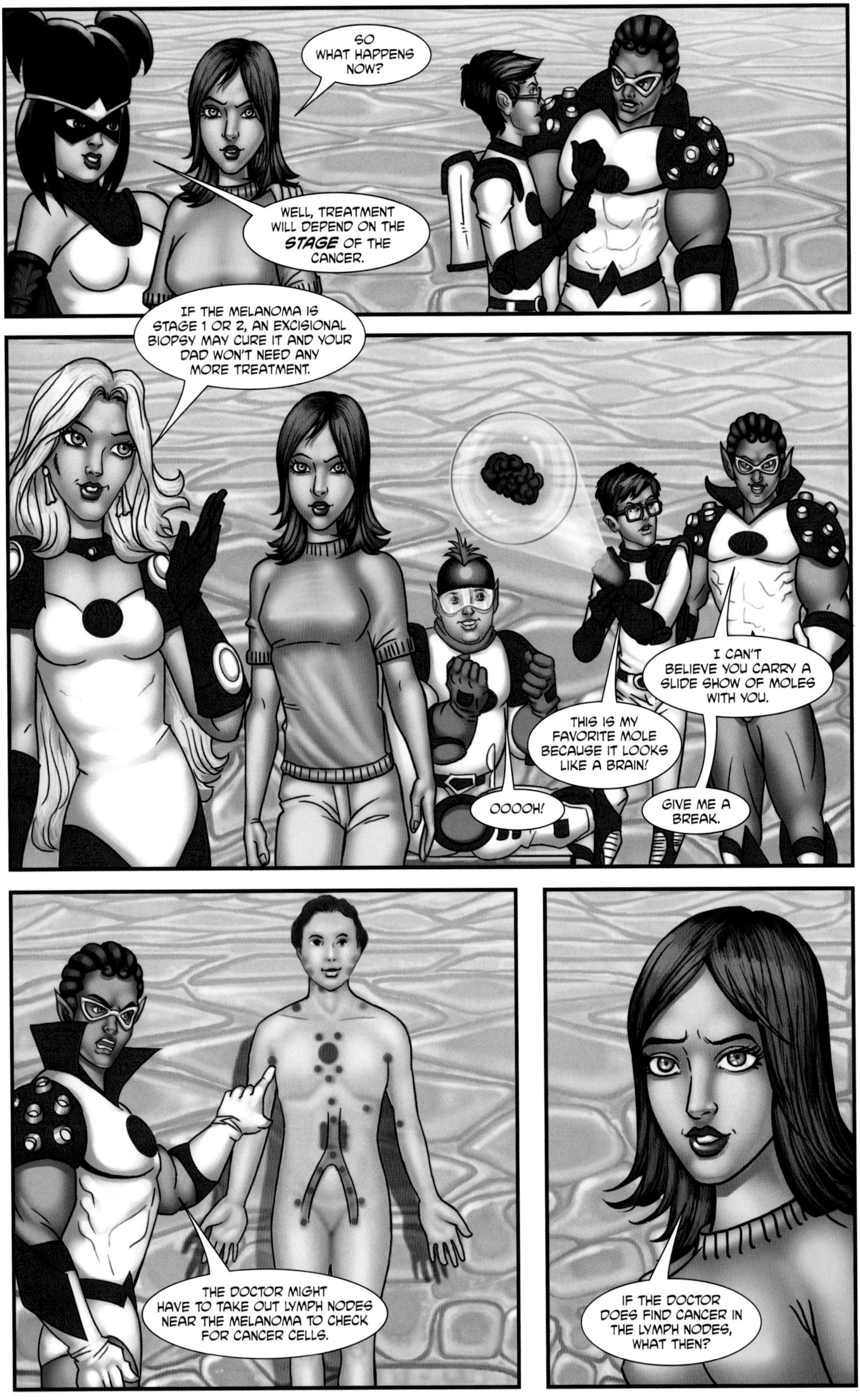
SO WHAT HAPPENS NOW?
WELL, TREATMENT WILL DEPEND ON THE STAGE OF THE CANCER.
IF THE MELANOMA IS STAGE 1 OR 2, AN EXCISIONAL BIOPSY MAY CURE IT AND YOUR DAD WON'T NEED ANY MORE TREATMENT.
THIS IS MY FAVORITE MOLE BECAUSE IT LOOKS LIKE A BRAIN!
OOOOH!
I CAN'T BELIEVE YOU CARRY A SLIDE SHOW OF MOLES WITH YOU.
GIVE ME A BREAK.
THE DOCTOR MIGHT HAVE TO TAKE OUT LYMPH NODES NEAR THE MELANOMA TO CHECK FOR CANCER CELLS.
IF THE DOCTOR DOES FIND CANCER IN THE LYMPH NODES, WHAT THEN?

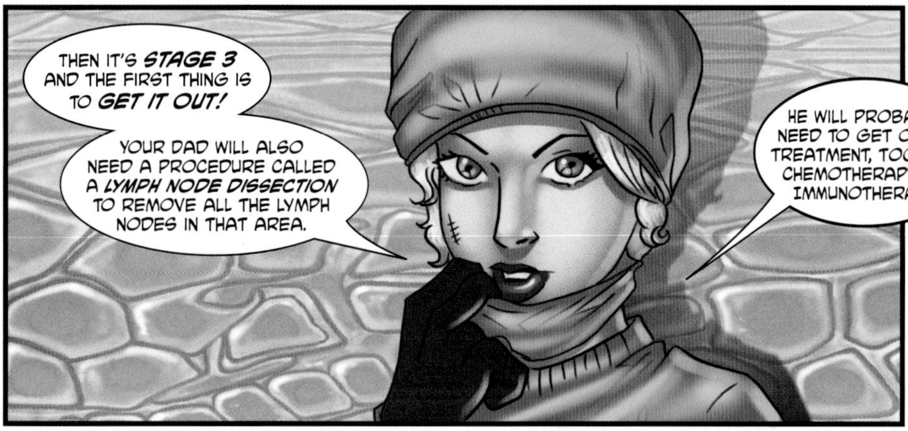
THEN IT'S STAGE 3 AND THE FIRST THING IS TO GET IT OUT!
YOUR DAD WILL ALSO NEED A PROCEDURE CALLED A LYMPH NODE DISSECTION TO REMOVE ALL THE LYMPH NODES IN THAT AREA.
HE WILL PROBABLY NEED TO GET OTHER TREATMENT, TOO, LIKE CHEMOTHERAPY OR IMMUNOTHERAPY.

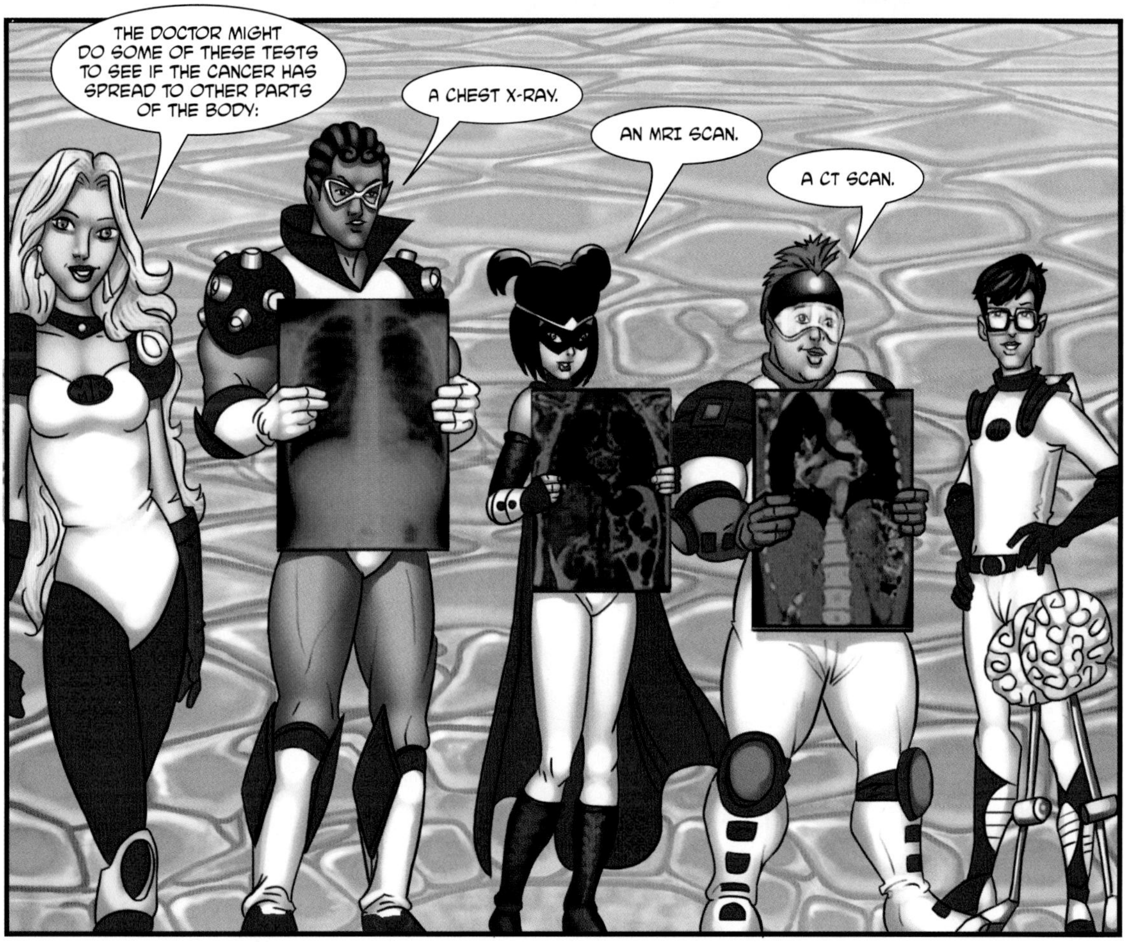
THE DOCTOR MIGHT DO SOME OF THESE TESTS TO SEE IF THE CANCER HAS SPREAD TO OTHER PARTS OF THE BODY:
A CHEST X-RAY.
AN MRI SCAN.
A CT SCAN.

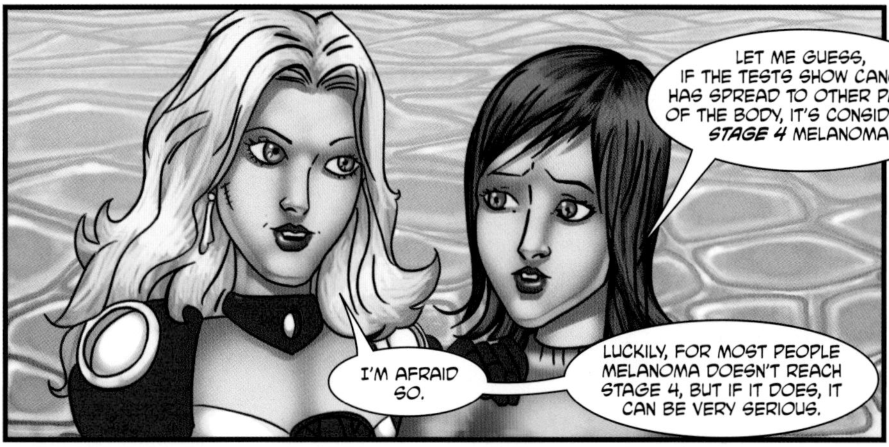
LET ME GUESS, IF THE TESTS SHOW CANCER HAS SPREAD TO OTHER PARTS OF THE BODY, IT'S CONSIDERED STAGE 4 MELANOMA.
I'M AFRAID SO.
LUCKILY, FOR MOST PEOPLE MELANOMA DOESN'T REACH STAGE 4, BUT IF IT DOES, IT CAN BE VERY SERIOUS.

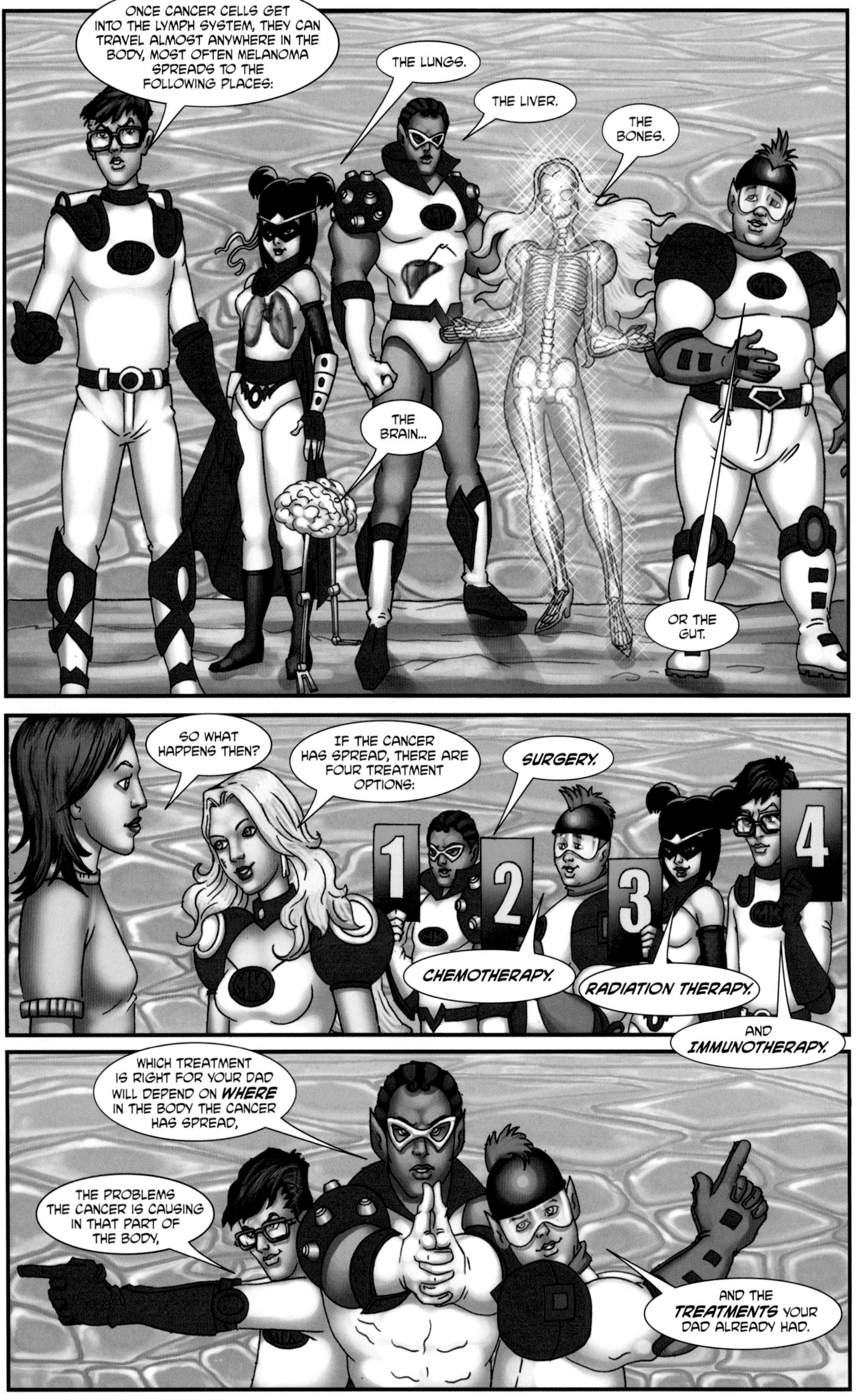

ONCE CANCER CELLS GET INTO THE LYMPH SYSTEM, THEY CAN TRAVEL ALMOST ANYWHERE IN THE BODY, MOST OFTEN MELANOMA SPREADS TO THE FOLLOWING PLACES:
THE LUNGS.
THE LIVER.
THE BONES.
THE BRAIN...
OR THE GUT.
SO WHAT HAPPENS THEN?
IF THE CANCER HAS SPREAD, THERE ARE FOUR TREATMENT OPTIONS:
1
SURGERY.
2
CHEMOTHERAPY.
3
RADIATION THERAPY.
4
AND IMMUNOTHERAPY.
WHICH TREATMENT IS RIGHT FOR YOUR DAD WILL DEPEND ON WHERE IN THE BODY THE CANCER HAS SPREAD,
THE PROBLEMS THE CANCER IS CAUSING IN THAT PART OF THE BODY,
AND THE TREATMENTS YOUR DAD ALREADY HAD.

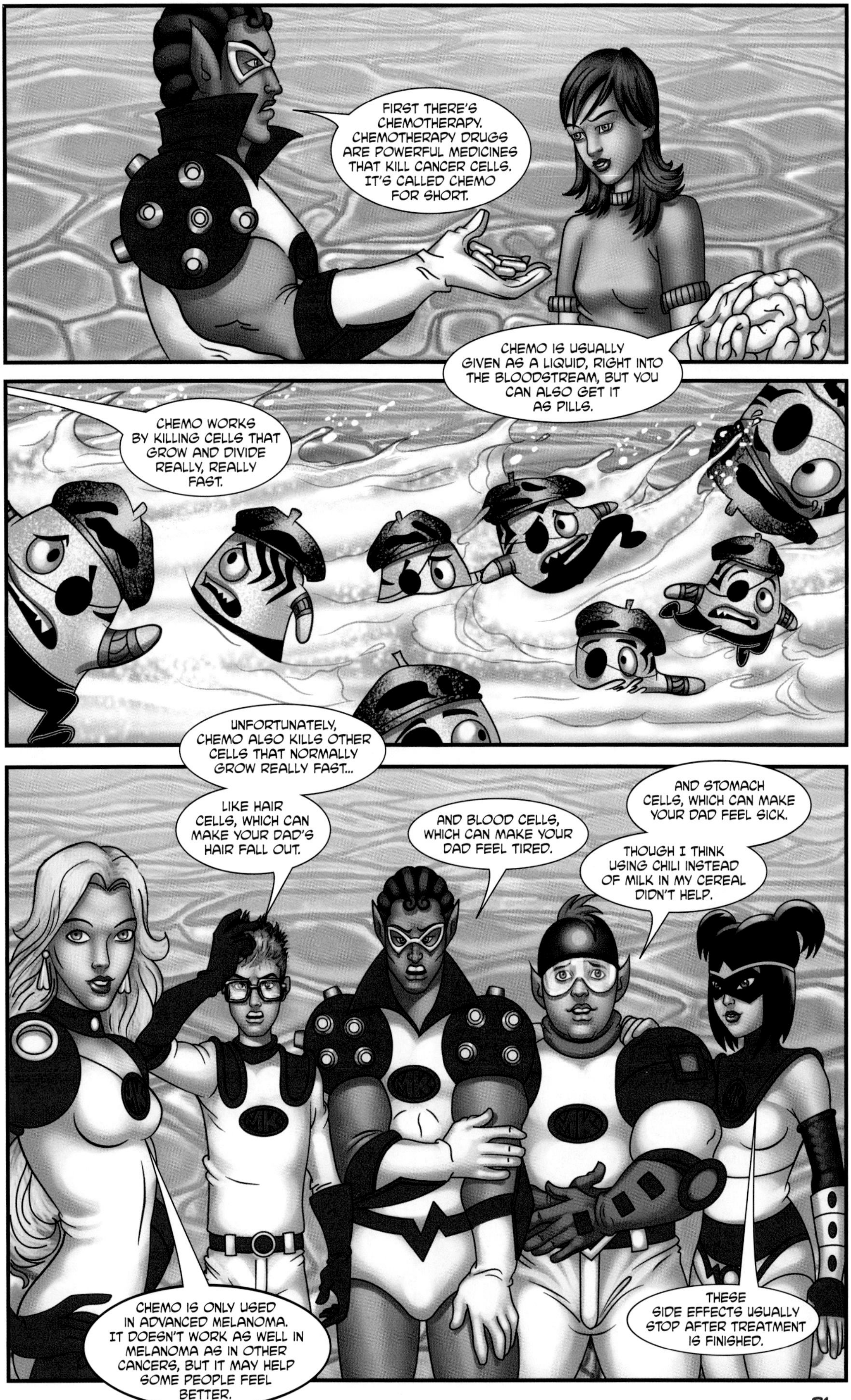
FIRST THERE'S CHEMOTHERAPY. CHEMOTHERAPY DRUGS ARE POWERFUL MEDICINES THAT KILL CANCER CELLS. IT'S CALLED CHEMO FOR SHORT.
CHEMO IS USUALLY GIVEN AS A LIQUID, RIGHT INTO THE BLOODSTREAM, BUT YOU CAN ALSO GET IT AS PILLS.
CHEMO WORKS BY KILLING CELLS THAT GROW AND DIVIDE REALLY, REALLY FAST.
UNFORTUNATELY, CHEMO ALSO KILLS OTHER CELLS THAT NORMALLY GROW REALLY FAST...
LIKE HAIR CELLS, WHICH CAN MAKE YOUR DAD'S HAIR FALL OUT.
AND BLOOD CELLS, WHICH CAN MAKE YOUR DAD FEEL TIRED.
AND STOMACH CELLS, WHICH CAN MAKE YOUR DAD FEEL SICK.
THOUGH I THINK USING CHILI INSTEAD OF MILK IN MY CEREAL DIDN'T HELP.
CHEMO IS ONLY USED IN ADVANCED MELANOMA. IT DOESN'T WORK AS WELL IN MELANOMA AS IN OTHER CANCERS, BUT IT MAY HELP SOME PEOPLE FEEL BETTER.
THESE SIDE EFFECTS USUALLY STOP AFTER TREATMENT IS FINISHED.

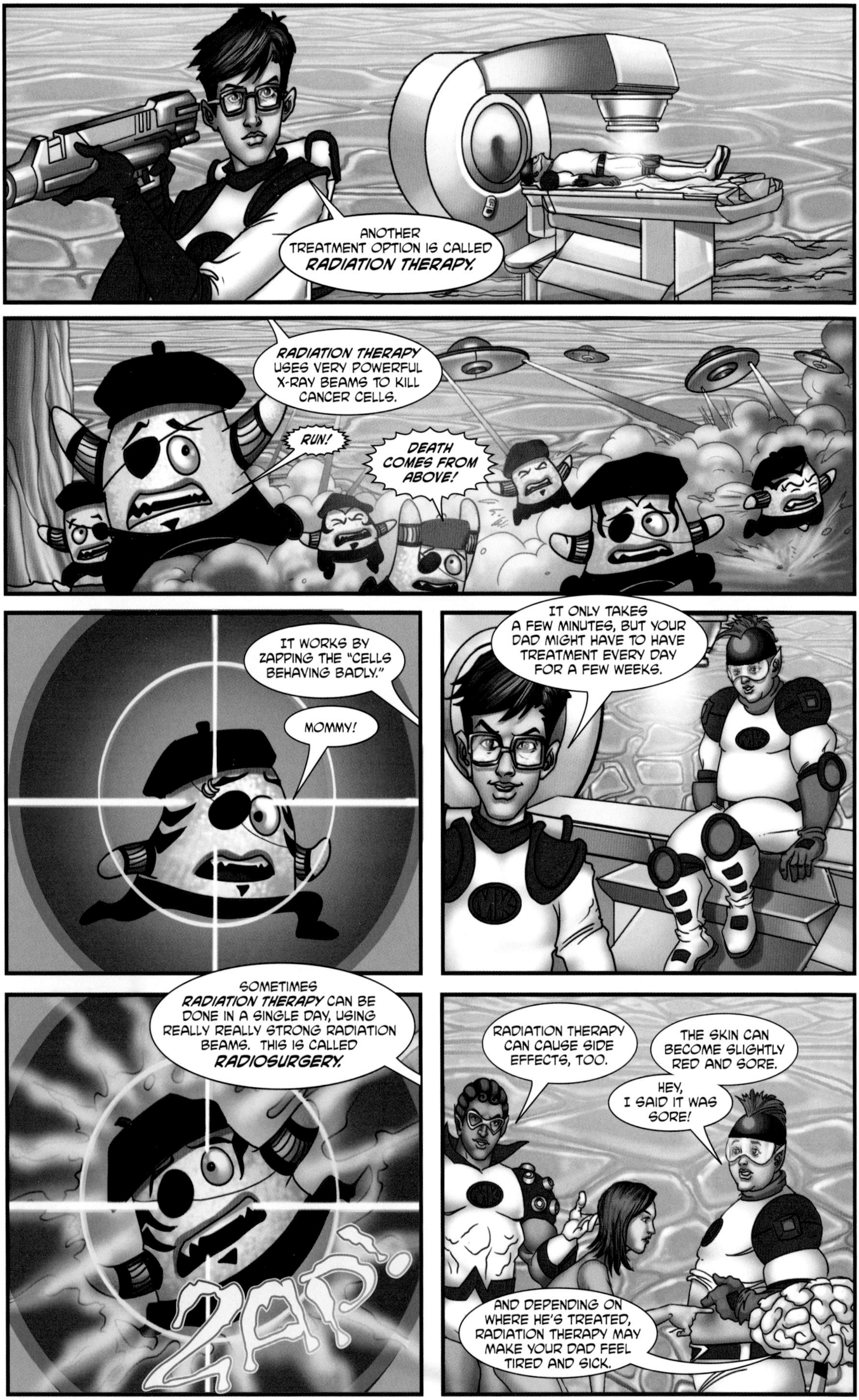
ANOTHER TREATMENT OPTION IS CALLED *RADIATION THERAPY.*
RADIATION THERAPY USES VERY POWERFUL X-RAY BEAMS TO KILL CANCER CELLS.
RUN!
DEATH COMES FROM ABOVE!
IT WORKS BY ZAPPING THE "CELLS BEHAVING BADLY."
MOMMY!
IT ONLY TAKES A FEW MINUTES, BUT YOUR DAD MIGHT HAVE TO HAVE TREATMENT EVERY DAY FOR A FEW WEEKS.
SOMETIMES *RADIATION THERAPY* CAN BE DONE IN A SINGLE DAY, USING REALLY REALLY STRONG RADIATION BEAMS. THIS IS CALLED ***RADIOSURGERY.***
ZAP!
RADIATION THERAPY CAN CAUSE SIDE EFFECTS, TOO.
THE SKIN CAN BECOME SLIGHTLY RED AND SORE.
HEY, I SAID IT WAS SORE!
AND DEPENDING ON WHERE HE'S TREATED, RADIATION THERAPY MAY MAKE YOUR DAD FEEL TIRED AND SICK.

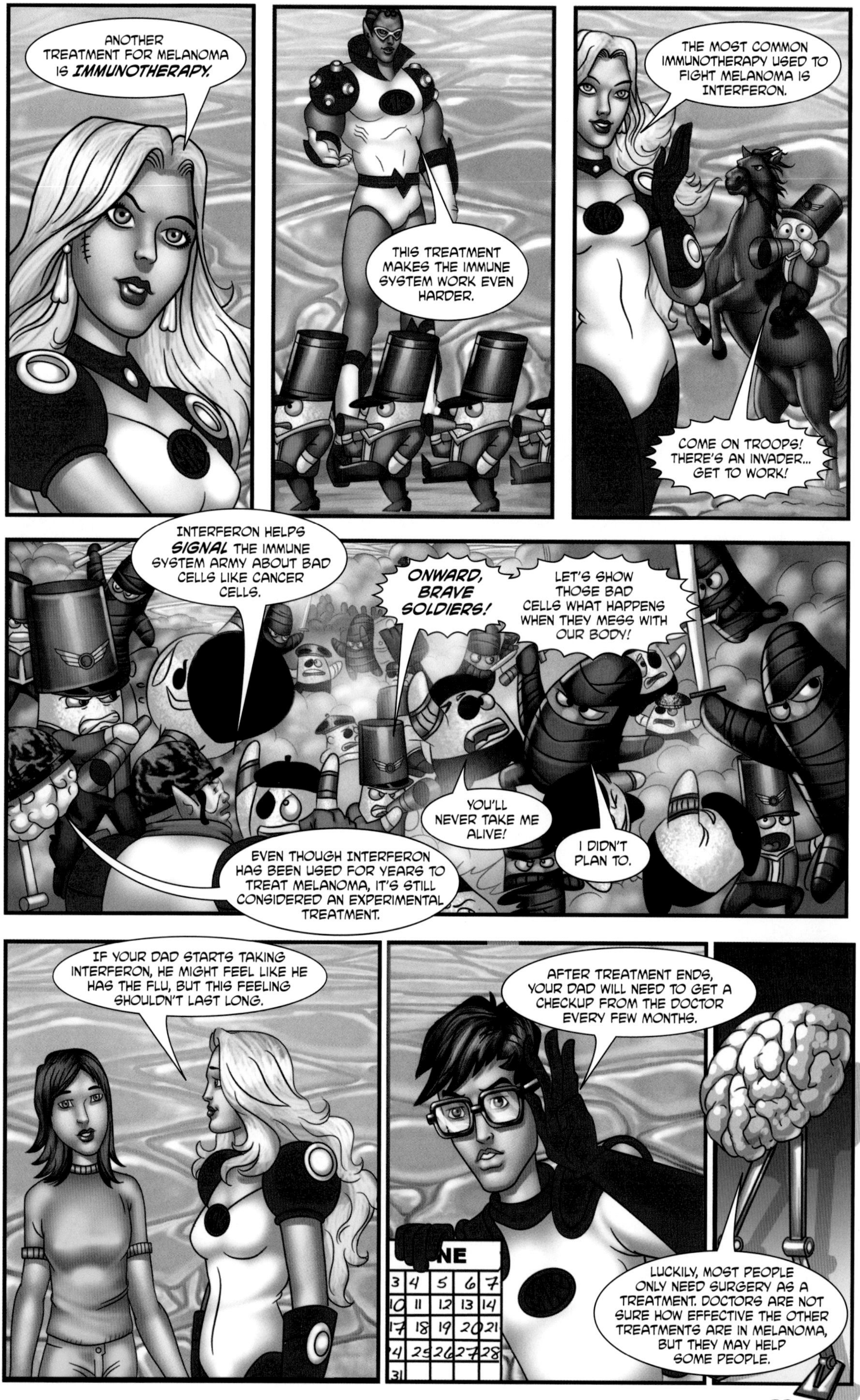
ANOTHER TREATMENT FOR MELANOMA IS *IMMUNOTHERAPY.*
THIS TREATMENT MAKES THE IMMUNE SYSTEM WORK EVEN HARDER.
THE MOST COMMON IMMUNOTHERAPY USED TO FIGHT MELANOMA IS INTERFERON.
COME ON TROOPS! THERE'S AN INVADER... GET TO WORK!
INTERFERON HELPS ***SIGNAL*** THE IMMUNE SYSTEM ARMY ABOUT BAD CELLS LIKE CANCER CELLS.
ONWARD, BRAVE SOLDIERS!
LET'S SHOW THOSE BAD CELLS WHAT HAPPENS WHEN THEY MESS WITH OUR BODY!
YOU'LL NEVER TAKE ME ALIVE!
I DIDN'T PLAN TO.
EVEN THOUGH INTERFERON HAS BEEN USED FOR YEARS TO TREAT MELANOMA, IT'S STILL CONSIDERED AN EXPERIMENTAL TREATMENT.
IF YOUR DAD STARTS TAKING INTERFERON, HE MIGHT FEEL LIKE HE HAS THE FLU, BUT THIS FEELING SHOULDN'T LAST LONG.
AFTER TREATMENT ENDS, YOUR DAD WILL NEED TO GET A CHECKUP FROM THE DOCTOR EVERY FEW MONTHS.
LUCKILY, MOST PEOPLE ONLY NEED SURGERY AS A TREATMENT. DOCTORS ARE NOT SURE HOW EFFECTIVE THE OTHER TREATMENTS ARE IN MELANOMA, BUT THEY MAY HELP SOME PEOPLE.

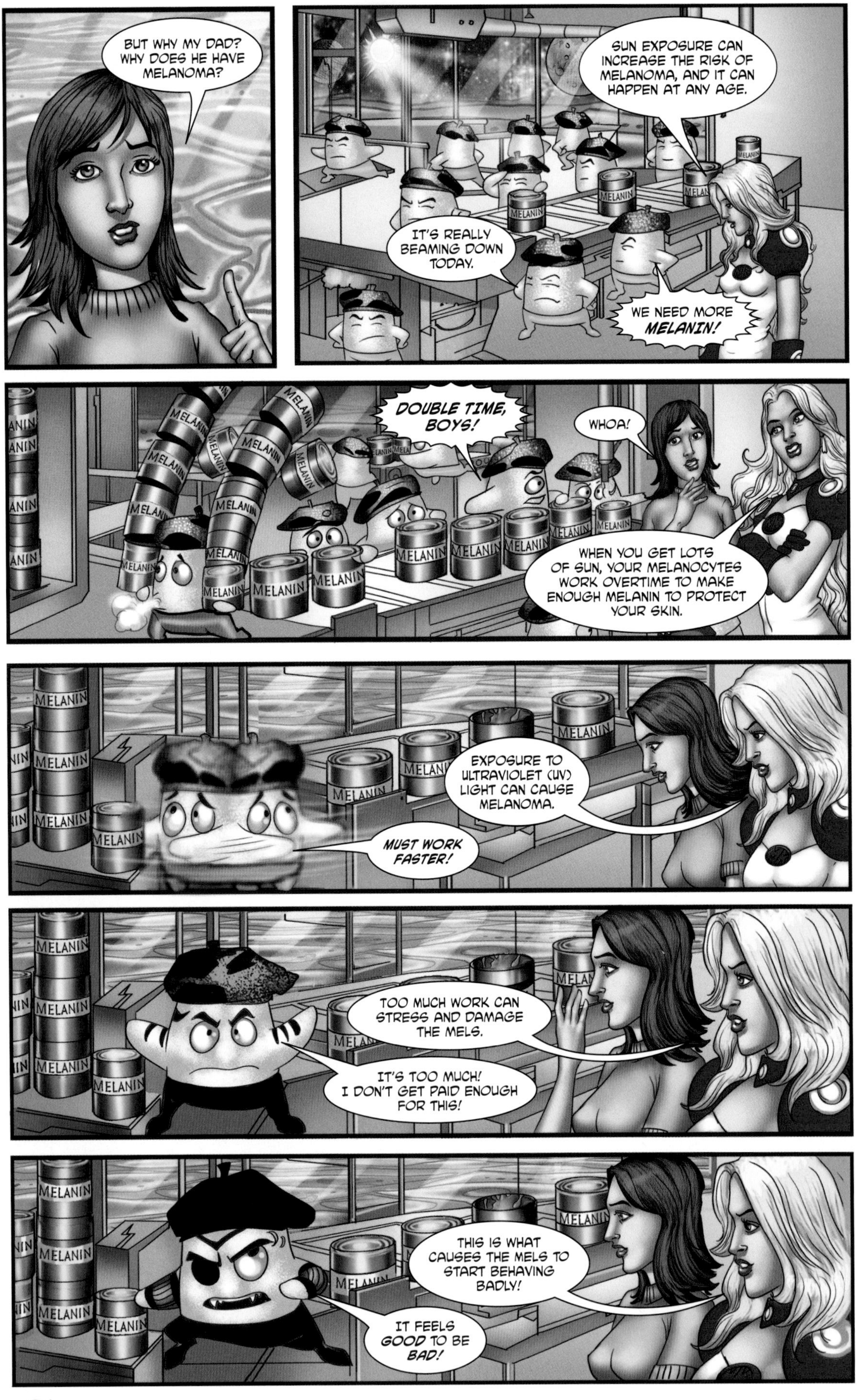
BUT WHY MY DAD? WHY DOES HE HAVE MELANOMA?
SUN EXPOSURE CAN INCREASE THE RISK OF MELANOMA, AND IT CAN HAPPEN AT ANY AGE.
IT'S REALLY BEAMING DOWN TODAY.
WE NEED MORE *MELANIN!*
DOUBLE TIME, BOYS!
WHOA!
WHEN YOU GET LOTS OF SUN, YOUR MELANOCYTES WORK OVERTIME TO MAKE ENOUGH MELANIN TO PROTECT YOUR SKIN.
EXPOSURE TO ULTRAVIOLET (UV) LIGHT CAN CAUSE MELANOMA.
MUST WORK FASTER!
TOO MUCH WORK CAN STRESS AND DAMAGE THE MELS.
IT'S TOO MUCH! I DON'T GET PAID ENOUGH FOR THIS!
THIS IS WHAT CAUSES THE MELS TO START BEHAVING BADLY!
IT FEELS *GOOD* TO BE *BAD!*

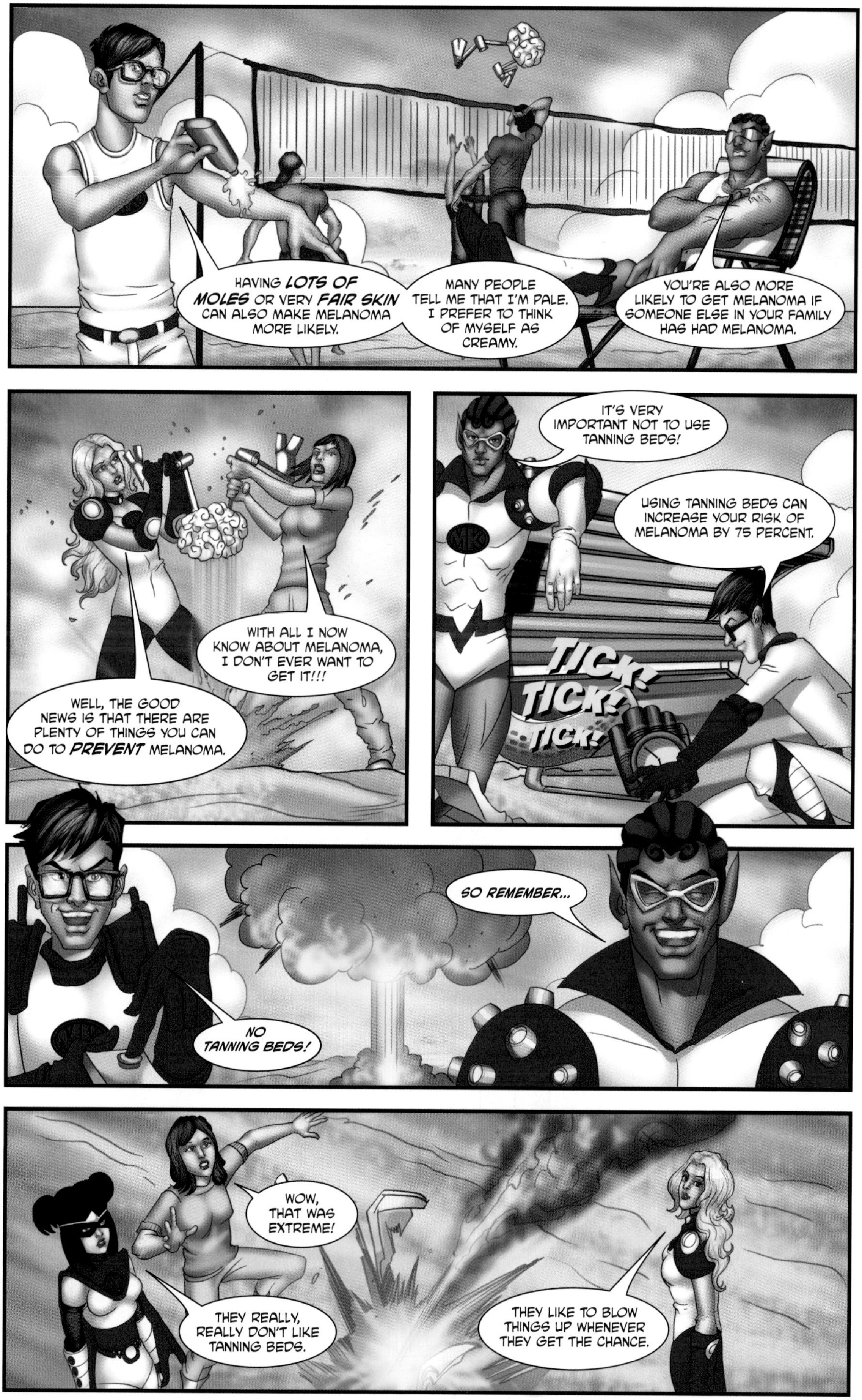
HAVING LOTS OF MOLES OR VERY FAIR SKIN CAN ALSO MAKE MELANOMA MORE LIKELY.
MANY PEOPLE TELL ME THAT I'M PALE. I PREFER TO THINK OF MYSELF AS CREAMY.
YOU'RE ALSO MORE LIKELY TO GET MELANOMA IF SOMEONE ELSE IN YOUR FAMILY HAS HAD MELANOMA.
WITH ALL I NOW KNOW ABOUT MELANOMA, I DON'T EVER WANT TO GET IT!!!
WELL, THE GOOD NEWS IS THAT THERE ARE PLENTY OF THINGS YOU CAN DO TO PREVENT MELANOMA.
IT'S VERY IMPORTANT NOT TO USE TANNING BEDS!
USING TANNING BEDS CAN INCREASE YOUR RISK OF MELANOMA BY 75 PERCENT.
TICK! TICK! TICK!
SO REMEMBER...
NO TANNING BEDS!
WOW, THAT WAS EXTREME!
THEY REALLY, REALLY DON'T LIKE TANNING BEDS.
THEY LIKE TO BLOW THINGS UP WHENEVER THEY GET THE CHANCE.

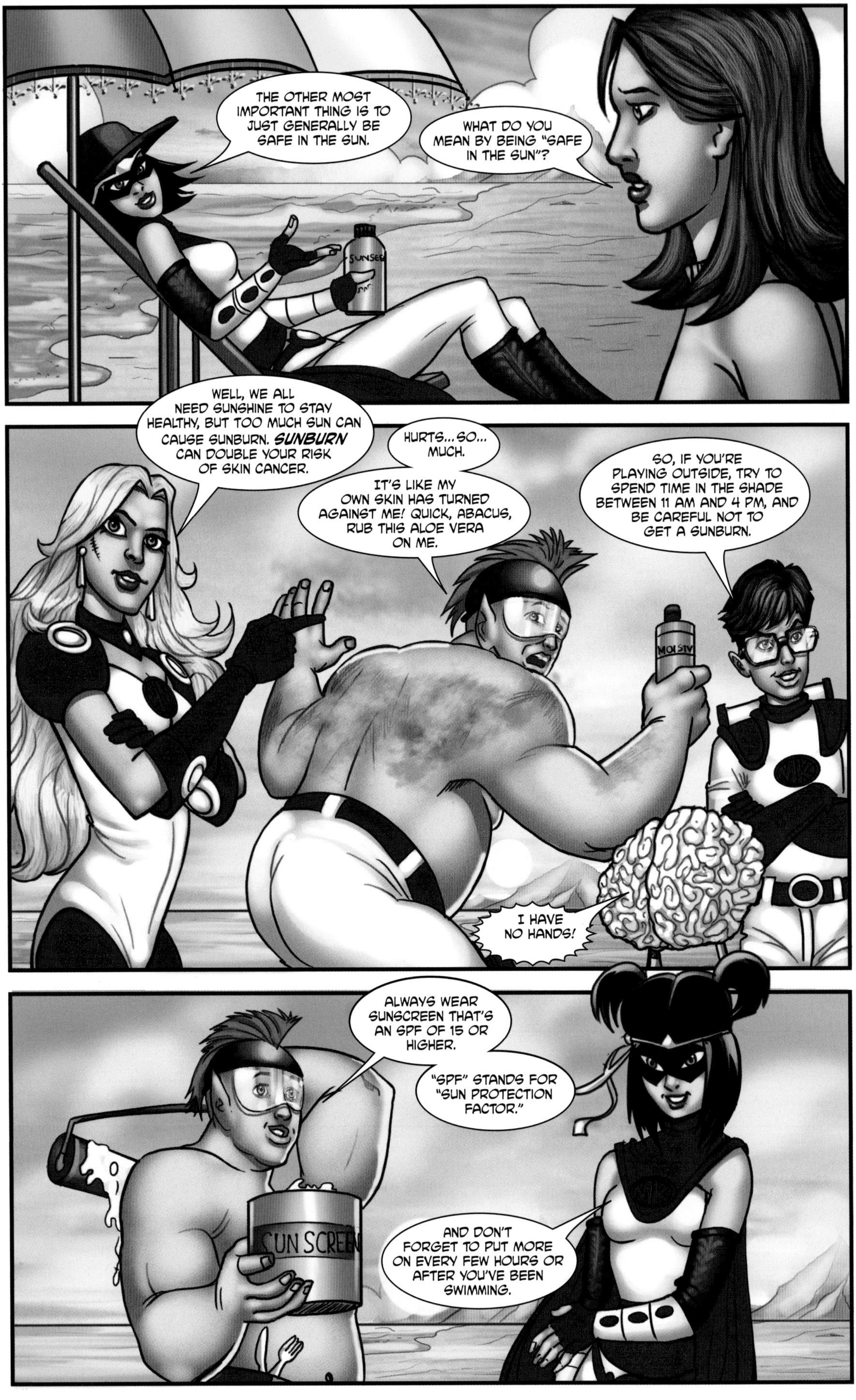
THE OTHER MOST IMPORTANT THING IS TO JUST GENERALLY BE SAFE IN THE SUN.
WHAT DO YOU MEAN BY BEING "SAFE IN THE SUN"?
SUNSC
WELL, WE ALL NEED SUNSHINE TO STAY HEALTHY, BUT TOO MUCH SUN CAN CAUSE SUNBURN. ***SUNBURN*** CAN DOUBLE YOUR RISK OF SKIN CANCER.
HURTS... SO... MUCH.
IT'S LIKE MY OWN SKIN HAS TURNED AGAINST ME! QUICK, ABACUS, RUB THIS ALOE VERA ON ME.
SO, IF YOU'RE PLAYING OUTSIDE, TRY TO SPEND TIME IN THE SHADE BETWEEN 11 AM AND 4 PM, AND BE CAREFUL NOT TO GET A SUNBURN.
MOISTU
I HAVE NO HANDS!
ALWAYS WEAR SUNSCREEN THAT'S AN SPF OF 15 OR HIGHER.
"SPF" STANDS FOR "SUN PROTECTION FACTOR."
SUN SCREEN
AND DON'T FORGET TO PUT MORE ON EVERY FEW HOURS OR AFTER YOU'VE BEEN SWIMMING.

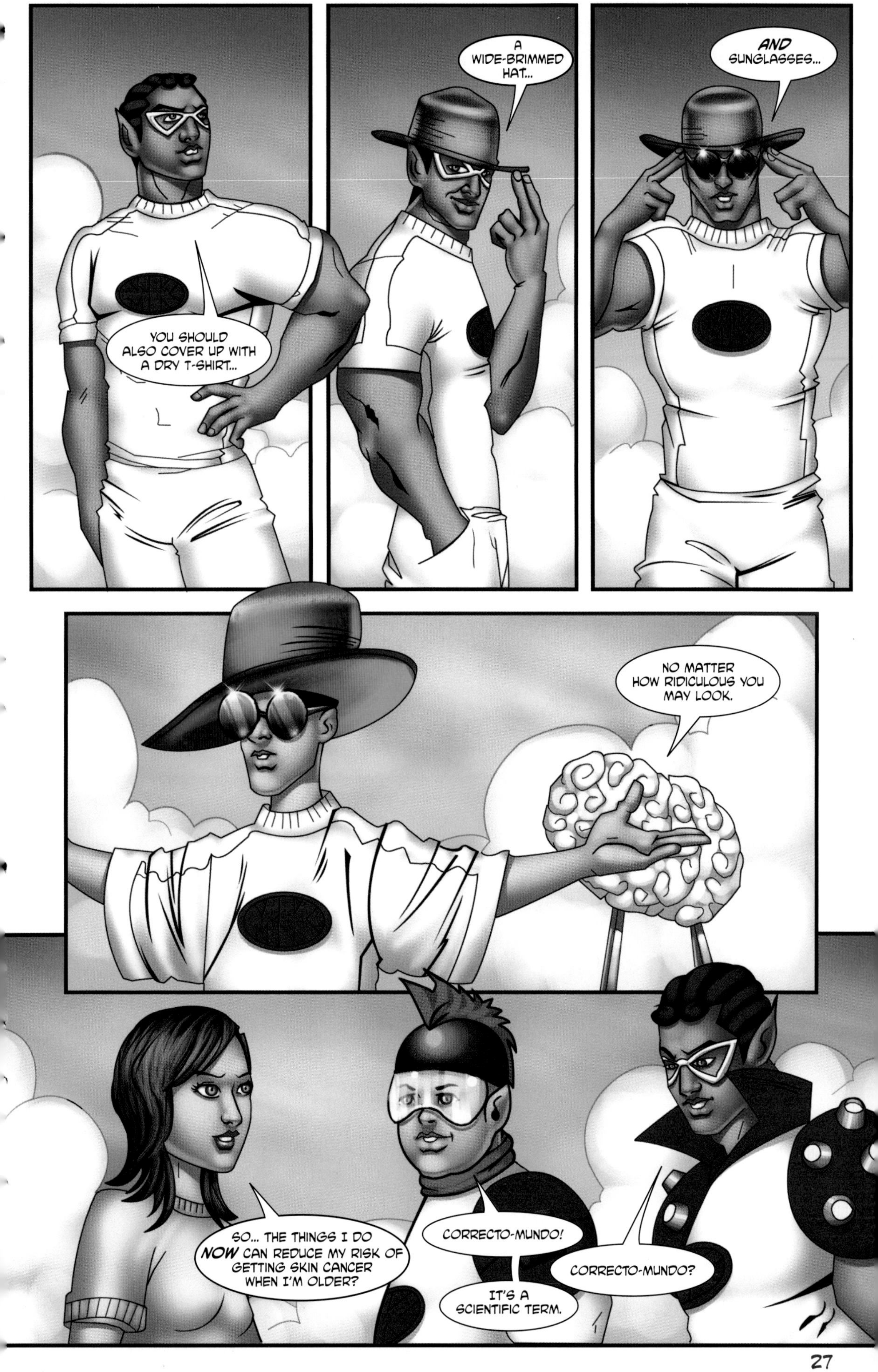
YOU SHOULD ALSO COVER UP WITH A DRY T-SHIRT...
A WIDE-BRIMMED HAT...
AND SUNGLASSES...
NO MATTER HOW RIDICULOUS YOU MAY LOOK.
SO... THE THINGS I DO NOW CAN REDUCE MY RISK OF GETTING SKIN CANCER WHEN I'M OLDER?
CORRECTO-MUNDO!
CORRECTO-MUNDO?
IT'S A SCIENTIFIC TERM.

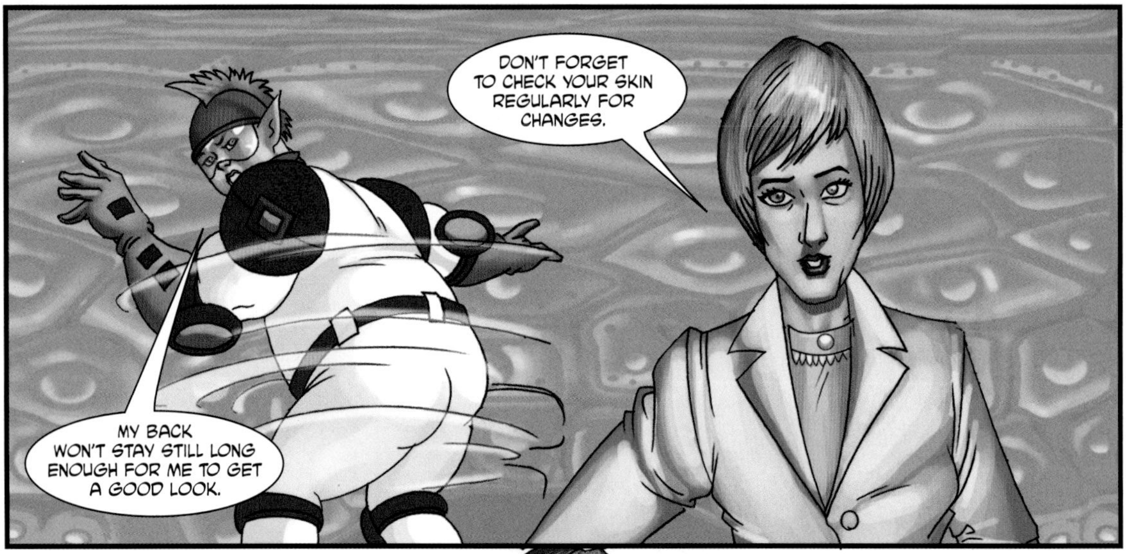
DON'T FORGET TO CHECK YOUR SKIN REGULARLY FOR CHANGES.
MY BACK WON'T STAY STILL LONG ENOUGH FOR ME TO GET A GOOD LOOK.

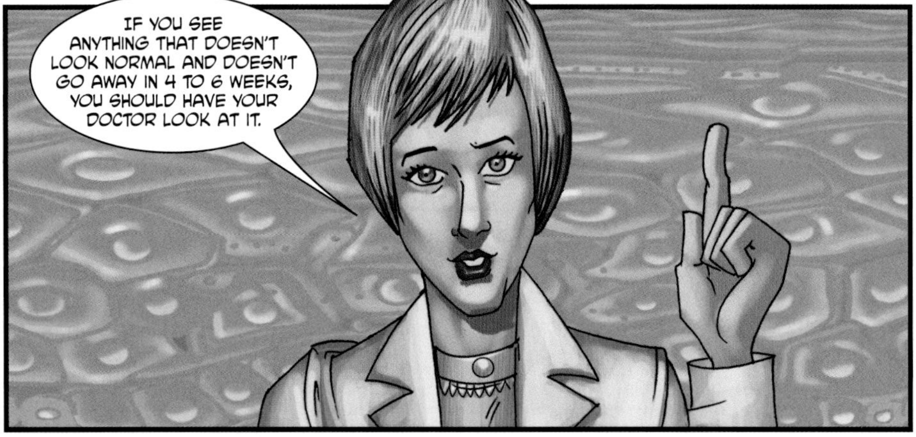
IF YOU SEE ANYTHING THAT DOESN'T LOOK NORMAL AND DOESN'T GO AWAY IN 4 TO 6 WEEKS, YOU SHOULD HAVE YOUR DOCTOR LOOK AT IT.

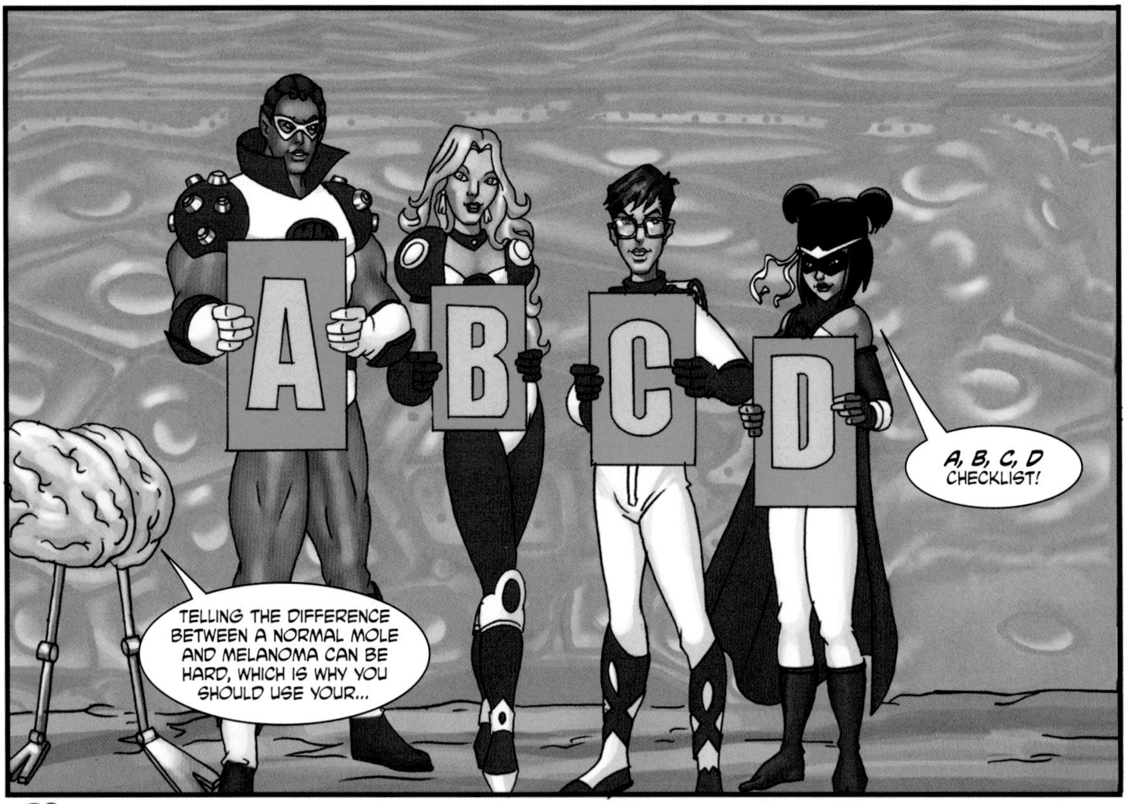
TELLING THE DIFFERENCE BETWEEN A NORMAL MOLE AND MELANOMA CAN BE HARD, WHICH IS WHY YOU SHOULD USE YOUR...
A
B
C
D
A, B, C, D CHECKLIST!

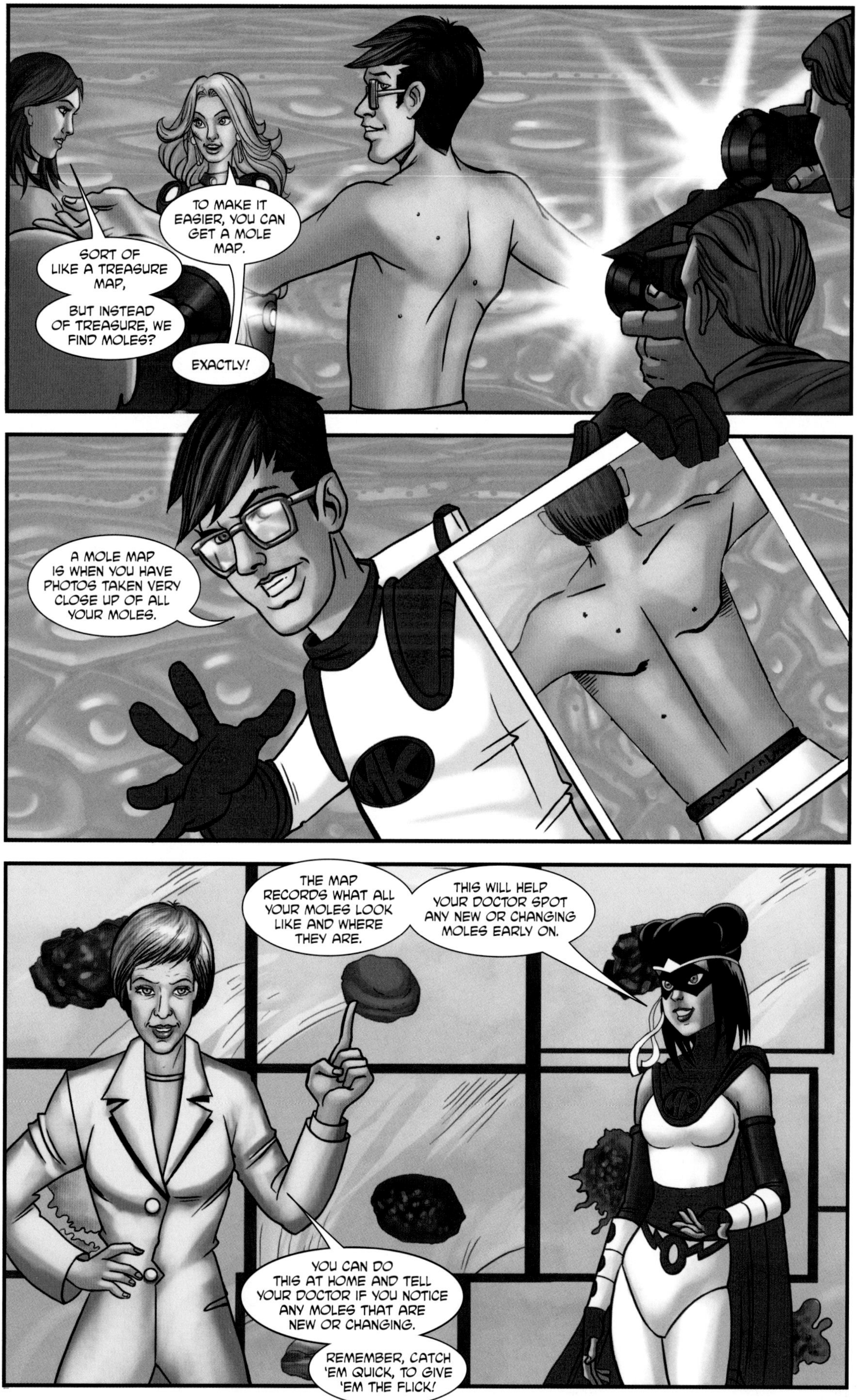
TO MAKE IT EASIER, YOU CAN GET A MOLE MAP.
SORT OF LIKE A TREASURE MAP,
BUT INSTEAD OF TREASURE, WE FIND MOLES?
EXACTLY!
A MOLE MAP IS WHEN YOU HAVE PHOTOS TAKEN VERY CLOSE UP OF ALL YOUR MOLES.
THE MAP RECORDS WHAT ALL YOUR MOLES LOOK LIKE AND WHERE THEY ARE.
THIS WILL HELP YOUR DOCTOR SPOT ANY NEW OR CHANGING MOLES EARLY ON.
YOU CAN DO THIS AT HOME AND TELL YOUR DOCTOR IF YOU NOTICE ANY MOLES THAT ARE NEW OR CHANGING.
REMEMBER, CATCH 'EM QUICK, TO GIVE 'EM THE FLICK!

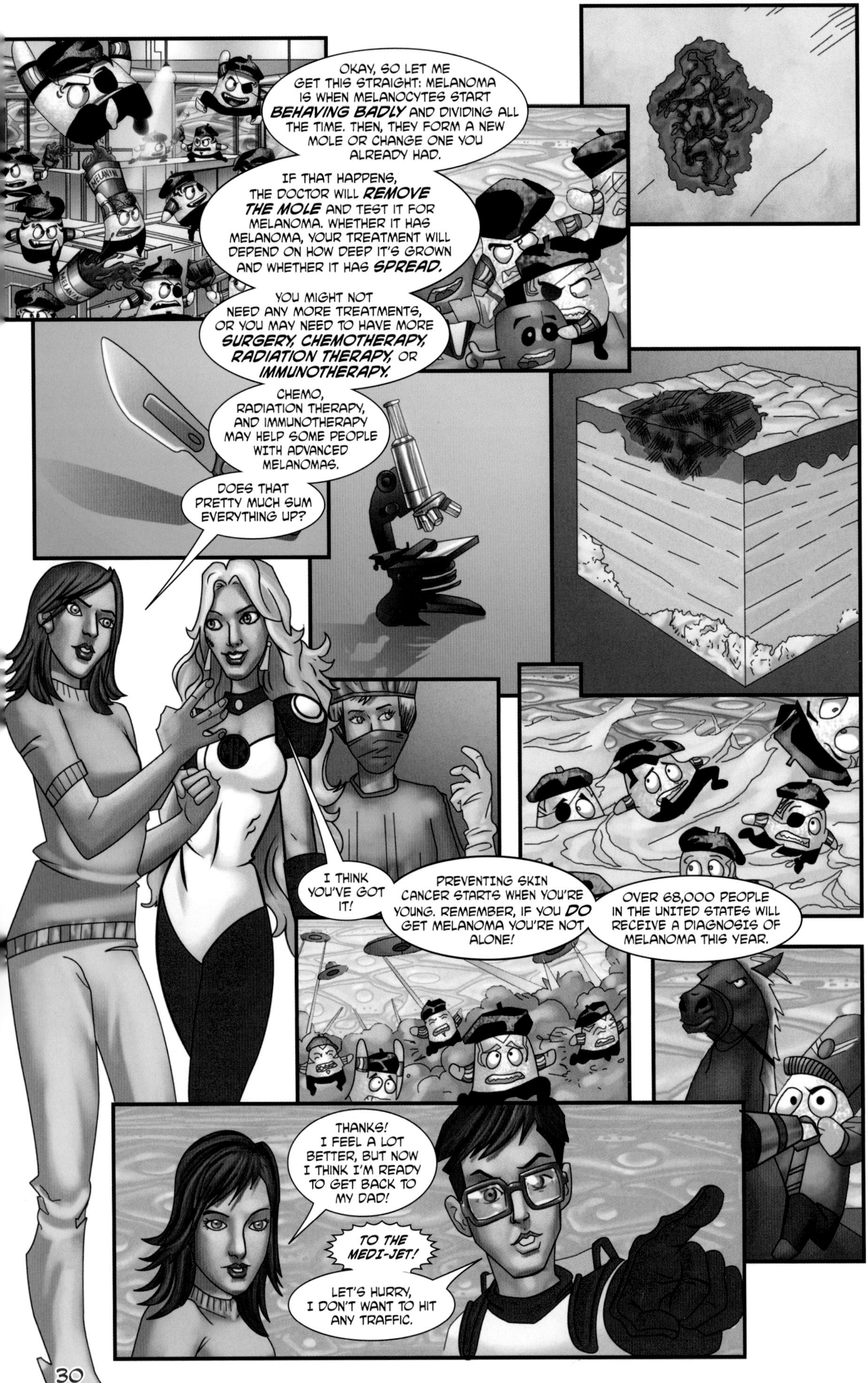
OKAY, SO LET ME GET THIS STRAIGHT: MELANOMA IS WHEN MELANOCYTES START BEHAVING BADLY AND DIVIDING ALL THE TIME. THEN, THEY FORM A NEW MOLE OR CHANGE ONE YOU ALREADY HAD.
IF THAT HAPPENS, THE DOCTOR WILL REMOVE THE MOLE AND TEST IT FOR MELANOMA. WHETHER IT HAS MELANOMA, YOUR TREATMENT WILL DEPEND ON HOW DEEP IT'S GROWN AND WHETHER IT HAS SPREAD.
YOU MIGHT NOT NEED ANY MORE TREATMENTS, OR YOU MAY NEED TO HAVE MORE SURGERY, CHEMOTHERAPY, RADIATION THERAPY, OR IMMUNOTHERAPY.
CHEMO, RADIATION THERAPY, AND IMMUNOTHERAPY MAY HELP SOME PEOPLE WITH ADVANCED MELANOMAS.
DOES THAT PRETTY MUCH SUM EVERYTHING UP?
I THINK YOU'VE GOT IT!
PREVENTING SKIN CANCER STARTS WHEN YOU'RE YOUNG. REMEMBER, IF YOU DO GET MELANOMA YOU'RE NOT ALONE!
OVER 68,000 PEOPLE IN THE UNITED STATES WILL RECEIVE A DIAGNOSIS OF MELANOMA THIS YEAR.
THANKS! I FEEL A LOT BETTER, BUT NOW I THINK I'M READY TO GET BACK TO MY DAD!
TO THE MEDI-JET!
LET'S HURRY, I DON'T WANT TO HIT ANY TRAFFIC.

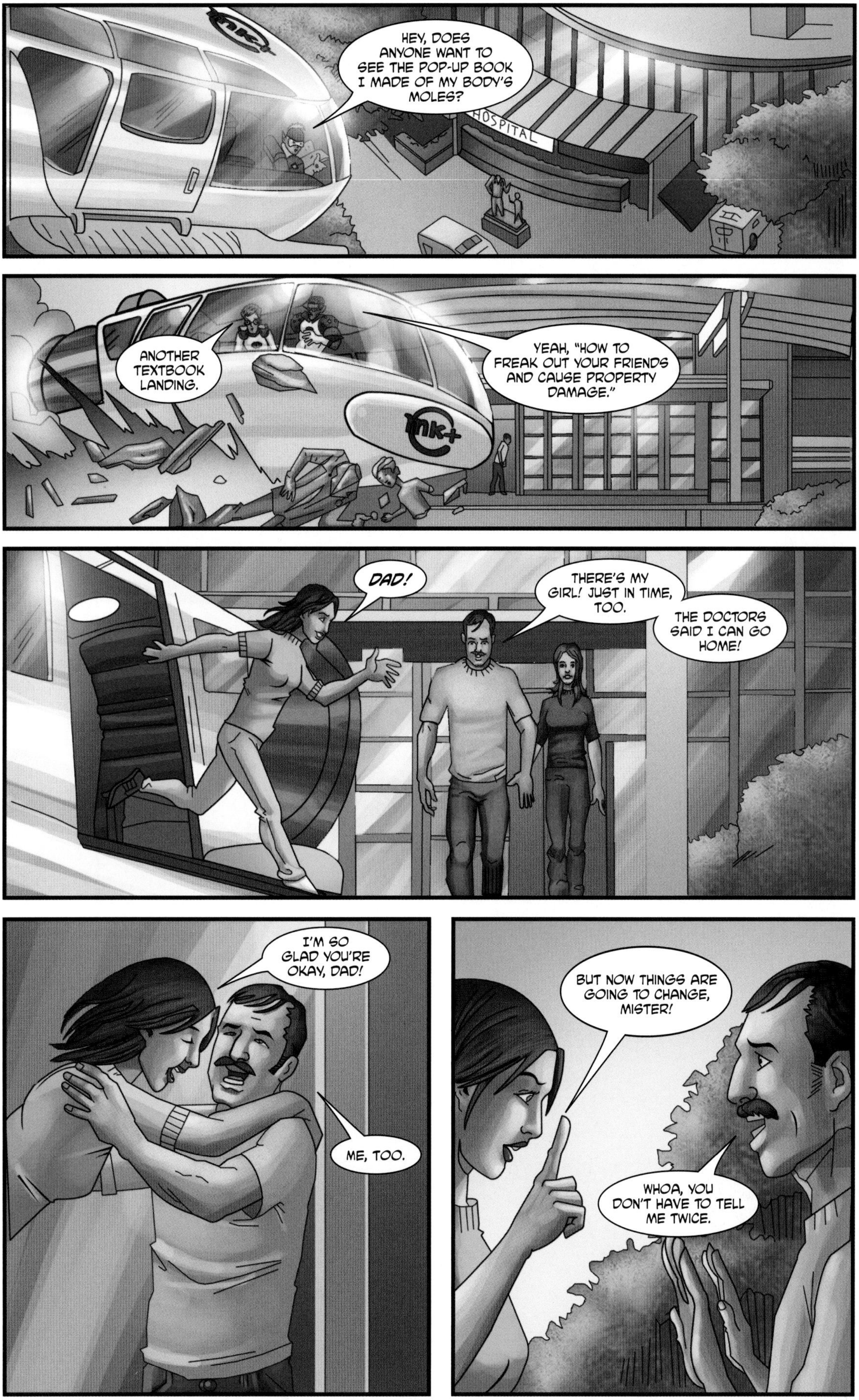
HEY, DOES ANYONE WANT TO SEE THE POP-UP BOOK I MADE OF MY BODY'S MOLES?
HOSPITAL
ANOTHER TEXTBOOK LANDING.
YEAH, "HOW TO FREAK OUT YOUR FRIENDS AND CAUSE PROPERTY DAMAGE."
DAD!
THERE'S MY GIRL! JUST IN TIME, TOO.
THE DOCTORS SAID I CAN GO HOME!
I'M SO GLAD YOU'RE OKAY, DAD!
ME, TOO.
BUT NOW THINGS ARE GOING TO CHANGE, MISTER!
WHOA, YOU DON'T HAVE TO TELL ME TWICE.

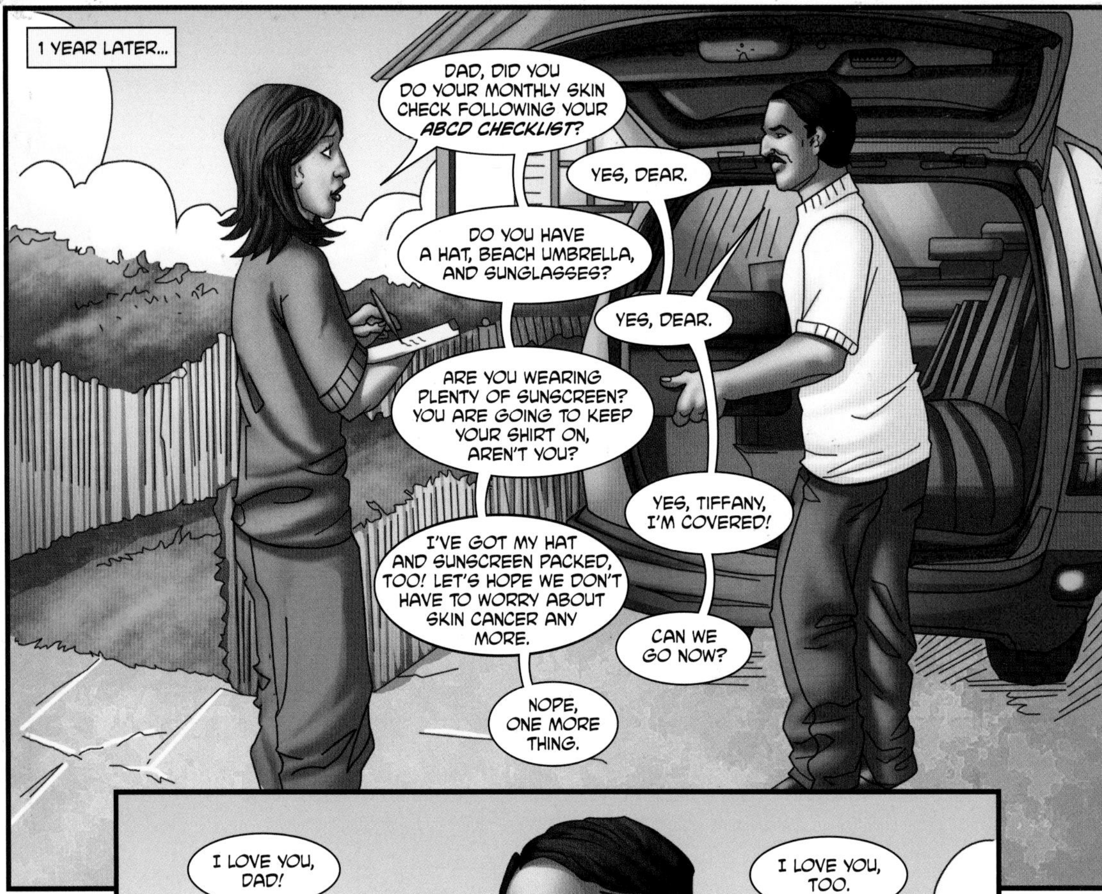
1 YEAR LATER...
DAD, DID YOU DO YOUR MONTHLY SKIN CHECK FOLLOWING YOUR *ABCD CHECKLIST*?
YES, DEAR.
DO YOU HAVE A HAT, BEACH UMBRELLA, AND SUNGLASSES?
YES, DEAR.
ARE YOU WEARING PLENTY OF SUNSCREEN? YOU ARE GOING TO KEEP YOUR SHIRT ON, AREN'T YOU?
YES, TIFFANY, I'M COVERED!
I'VE GOT MY HAT AND SUNSCREEN PACKED, TOO! LET'S HOPE WE DON'T HAVE TO WORRY ABOUT SKIN CANCER ANY MORE.
CAN WE GO NOW?
NOPE, ONE MORE THING.

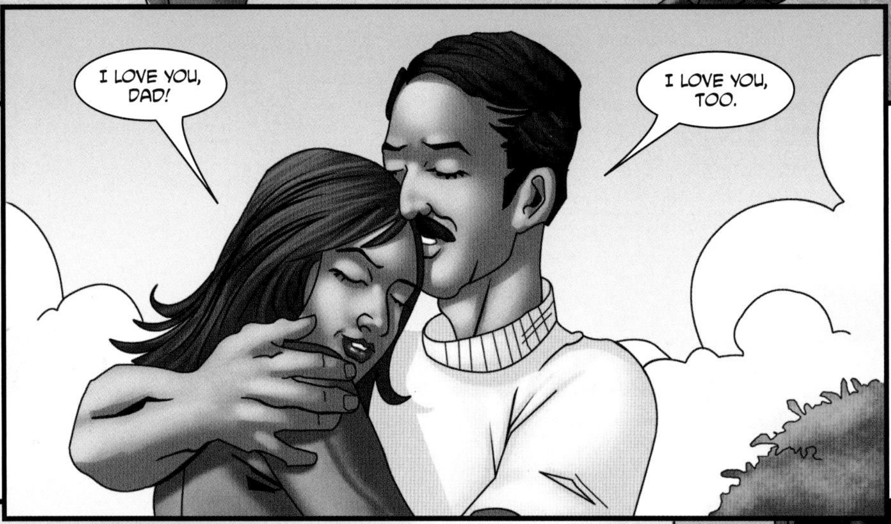
I LOVE YOU, DAD!
I LOVE YOU, TOO.

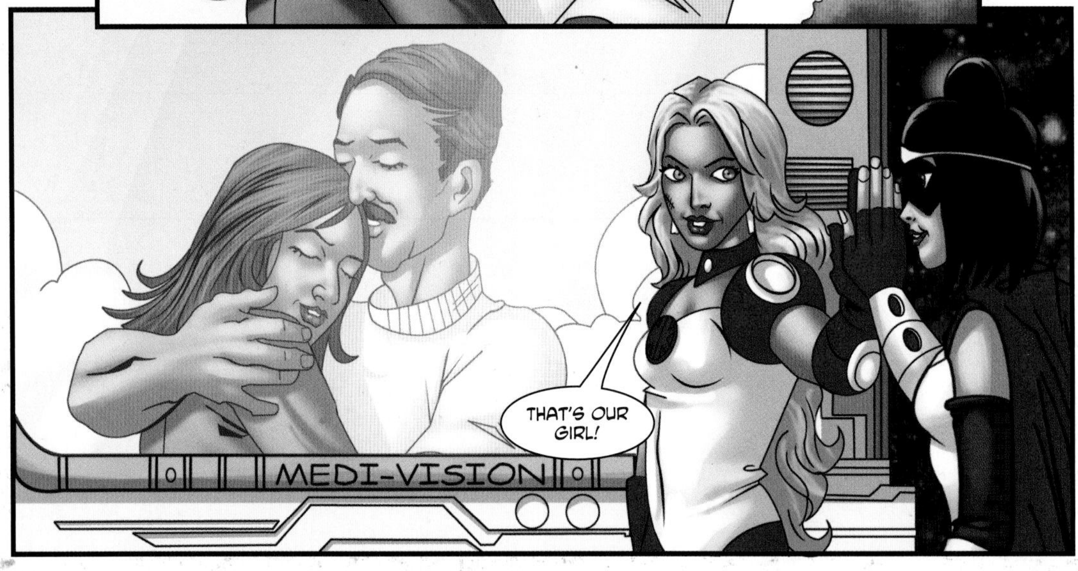
THAT'S OUR GIRL!
MEDI-VISION